Loving Me, Blocking Them

A *Young Woman's* Guide to
Texting, Dating, and Breaking Up

Michelle Parizon

Loving Me, Blocking Them

Copyright © 2020 by Michelle Parizon

Outer Vision Publishing
www.lovingmeblockingthem.com
www.outervisionpublishing.com

All rights reserved. No part of this publication may be reproduced, stored in a retrieval system, or transmitted, in any form or by any means, electronic, mechanical, photocopying, recording, or otherwise, without the prior written permission of the author.

This book is not intended to take the place of medical advice from a trained medical professional. Readers are advised to consult a physician or other qualified health professional regarding treatment of their medical problems. Neither the publisher nor the author takes any responsibility for any possible consequences from any treatment, action, or application of medicine, herb, or preparation to any person reading or following the information in this book.

ISBN: 978-1-7370449-0-1

Edited by Alex Cruden

Back cover photograph by Bryana Williams
Cover design by Digital Detroit Media

Printed in the United States of America

This book is dedicated to the understanding that your destiny is guided by the choices you make as you rise into your future.

TABLE OF CONTENTS

FOREWORD vii

INTRODUCTION ix

LESSON 1: ASSESS SO YOU WON'T BE A MESS 1

LESSON 2: WIDE OPEN! KEEP YOUR EYES AND EARS OPEN 10

LESSON 3: YOU DON'T HAVE TO TWERK IT TO WORK IT! 27

LESSON 4: LEVEL UP! WHAT LEVEL ARE YOU ON? 35

LESSON 5: BEING TOO NEEDY CAN MAKE YOU SEEM GREEDY 39

LESSON 6: HOW **YOU** MAKE A PLAYER 44

LESSON 7: HE IS WHO HE IS 59

LESSON 8: HE'S NOT YOUR DADDY, AND YOU ARE NOT HIS MAMA!.... 71

LESSON 9: THE RELATIONSHIP SCALE: YOU'RE AT A 5, BUT HE'S AT A 1 . 76

LESSON 10: READING THE SIGNS OF "I'M OUT!" 81

LESSON 11: THE BOOMERANG EFFECT:
    WHEN GUYS TRY TO COME BACK 86

LESSON 12: SO, HOW IS THAT WORKING FOR YOU?
    TAKING ADVICE FROM THE WRONG PEOPLE 91

LESSON 13: WHO'S INTO YOU? 96

LESSON 14: REALITY TV IS NOT YOUR REALITY 101

LESSON 15: IS YOUR LIFE AN OPEN BOOK? 105

LESSON 16: HEAR WHAT HE SAYS, WATCH WHAT HE DOES 115

LESSON 17: DON'T GET TRAPPED WITH SOCIAL MEDIA
           AND EXPLICIT FLICKS......................................116

LESSON 18: YOU MUST BE INTO CRYIN' IF YOU BELIEVE HIS LYIN' 122

LESSON 19: DON'T I KNOW YOU FROM SOMEWHERE?
           DATING THE SAME TYPE OVER AND OVER 126

LESSON 20: DRAMA ADDICTS 128

LESSON 21: YOLO: WHAT MAKES YOU HAPPY?..............................143

ACKNOWLEDGEMENTS 145

FOREWORD

Loving Me, Blocking Them is a roadmap for today's teenage and adult young women on how to navigate through their relationships with the opposite sex. Each chapter, which the author refers to as a "Lesson," is presented in a warm, concise, easy-to-read, non-preachy, often-humorous manner.

Michelle Parizon, an educator to her core, offers self-assessment quizzes, thought-provoking scenarios, helpful examples, and colorful anecdotes. The way she writes is a like a conversation that goes straight to the heart.

There are so many valuable lessons in this book! I will highlight a few of my favorites, probably because a couple of these lessons were the most difficult for me to learn.

I love the "slow your roll" lesson. It contains a Four-Week Assessment Tool, which teaches you to ask the right questions, make accurate observations, and have realistic expectations about how your relationship is evolving—all so that you will not barrel full steam ahead with your "eyes wide shut."

Michelle warns us that if you don't get your lessons while you are young, you'll keep repeating them until you do. Fortunately, I did finally learn many of the lessons Michelle puts forth, but it was not without hard knocks. Those of you who are wise enough to adopt the suggested tools and internalize the lessons contained in this book will, no doubt, save yourselves the agony of many broken hearts and, maybe, even years of despair, depression, and anxiety.

If you think I'm exaggerating about the years of suffering that you can endure, if you don't get these lessons now, I can introduce you to several attractive, well-educated girlfriends with successful careers in their 50s and even 60s who are unhappy, frustrated, bitter, and emotionally drained because they still determine their self-worth based upon the attention of a man.

Another important point Michelle makes is to wisely choose what you share with others. As she says, "You can't tell everyone everything!" Know whom you can trust and can confide in so that your personal business doesn't end up all over your school, office, or even worse social media. Michelle cautions everyone to think about the consequences of posting illicit pictures and hateful messages before you hit the send button. Once it is out there, it can haunt you for life.

Having had discussions and interviews with numerous young men, Michelle also gives us invaluable insights into how males look at the world and their perspectives on young women. Although females are encouraged to empower themselves, it is not by diminishing the power of young men. Michelle teaches us that power is not gained at the expense of others, but that true power is an inside job.

In any case, without a doubt, the most valuable lesson, one that runs throughout the book, is that we, as women, must know our own self-worth. Loving ourselves, being comfortable in our own skin, learning to be alone without being lonely are life lessons that, when learned, will enrich not only our own lives but also the lives of everyone we know and love.

Loving Me, Blocking Them pulses with wisdom and good advice. I wish there had been a book like this when I was coming of age. It could have saved me from many days of woeful despondency. Do yourself a favor and read this book!

—*Myra Anderson, retired educator, mother of Big Sean, and President and CEO of the Sean Anderson Foundation.*

INTRODUCTION

Are you laughing right now? Are you crying? Are you torn between saying yes to a special guy and stomping away? If you answered yes to any of these questions you are not alone. Dealing with guys isn't always easy. In fact, it can be downright confusing—especially when in you're in your teens or twenties.

This is a tough stage in life. You're either going on hot dates or stressing over tough exams. You're getting ready for prom, prepping for college, or interviewing for your first big job. You're making decisions about hair, clothes, schools, careers, makeup and, yes, guys.

OK, who are we kidding? Especially guys.

Somehow you can't get them out of your mind, can you? What's worse, you can't seem to figure them out. Why?

Well, for one thing, your focus is in the wrong place. Instead of putting all your attention on that cute guy at school or work, you should have your mind on something else.

Yourself.

Knowing yourself is just as important—in fact more important—than knowing others. But there you go, trying to figure him out, REALLY into trying to make things work, but things keep going wrong. What is the problem? Why doesn't he get it? After all, you're doing everything to be the perfect girlfriend. You are being a good listener. You help him with his homework. In fact, sometimes you even do his homework for him. You are affectionate. You go places with him even when you are not interested in going. Honestly, you are doing everything you can think of to keep him happy. Yet things between the two of you are not working out as you had hoped and planned.

The problem is this: You're chasing the wrong guy and doing it for the wrong reasons. In most cases, you don't even know the real reason.

Throughout the years, countless teenage and slightly older girls—and guys—have come to me to talk about their relationship issues. This simply started happening and I'm not exactly sure why. I guess I'm approachable. Maybe it was because I treated these young people as if they were my own children, and I listened, and I was honest and direct.

This has been going on for so long now that I have come to expect it. It seems like a steady stream of young people stop by my classroom desk at school, pull some chairs over and ask me to guide them through the process of dating, texting, and breaking up. Sometimes we have lunch while we talk. My paid job is to be an English teacher in Detroit—high school and community college—but I also seem to serve as the school mom.

These young people seek out my wisdom the same way I used to seek out the wisdom of my elders. In the old days, we even had a tradition of passing down family values, mottos and advice from great grandmothers to grandmothers to mothers and daughters.

Unfortunately, this tradition is dying. So, I decided to do the next best thing. Since so many young people gather around me, asking the same questions, I began to compile my answers in a special journal that I felt would come in handy one day. This book is the result of that effort. I was fortunate to have had a cluster of mature, insightful women who offered guidance on dating and relationships. Through this book I hope to do the same. I wrote it to support you on your journey to becoming a confident, strong, wise, young woman so that as you mature you will have a better handle on dealing with the opposite sex.

While it is my hope that you will enjoy learning from this book, there will be things said at some point that you will totally disagree with and won't want to hear. I get it, and that's OK. Just remember, something that you may not like could still be true. It is my hope that you honor your life by realizing that you matter, and that you see value in yourself and that you have high standards as you make the best possible dating decisions.

Lesson 1

ASSESS SO YOU WON'T BE A MESS

He's hot. He has a big, sexy smile. He's got swag. But is he the right guy for you?

There's nothing wrong with being directly attracted to someone as long as you don't go overboard before you know whether the guy is worth your time, or worthy of you. But sometimes when you're in that zone of really wanting to date, better judgment can fall by the wayside. Before you know it, your emotions are spiraling out of control. You have become so determined to have someone in your life that you make missteps that can cause you to lose sight of who you are, and where you're going. Guys are great, but when the need to be with them begins to dominate your life, you should consider thoroughly reassessing the situation. Waiting 30 days before diving in full force will give you the opportunity to make observations about certain attitudes and behaviors that you may overlook if you're moving too fast.

Let's look at a common scenario. You have met a guy and are quickly attracted to him. Perhaps it is his charm, or that he is *fine*. And, even better, he seems to have a *dope* personality. He asks you for your number or offers to give you his. As soon as his interest in you is confirmed, you go into **emotional takeoff.** Before you know it, you're all in. You immediately have high hopes and expectations about what this brief encounter has the potential to become. You barely know the guy's last name, and already you are planning your future together.

SLOW YOUR ROLL! You need to get a handle—a serious grip—on your emotions. At this point, you really don't know if this guy is worth you, your time, or even how seriously he wants to invest time in you. Maybe you were introduced by a mutual acquaintance, but you can't take someone else's word for how great he is. You really need to make your own assessment. You need to keep your heart, your secrets, and your treasures under wrap until you see who he really is.

Now, if you think these suggestions are for someone slower and less perceptive than you ... pause and take a deep breath. Think long and hard before you decide I'm wrong.

If we were sitting face-to-face you might be asking me: "Do you really expect me to wait 30 days before I let this guy know that I really like him? Do you know how long I have been waiting to meet the right guy? Don't you realize that 30 days is way too long to wait before letting a guy know you're interested, and available? Are you for real? What if he moves on to someone else before the 30 days are up?"

Well, let's back up. I am not suggesting that you wait 30 days to let him know you are interested. I am only suggesting that you exercise some self-control and slow yourself down long enough to really learn about the other person, which you can only do if you give yourself a bit of time to do your due diligence. **You need to assess so you won't be a mess!**

First, if he moves on to someone else that quickly (before the 30 days have expired), he wasn't sincerely interested in you in the first place. You should NEVER make yourself too accessible to a guy before you know where HE'S coming from! In many instances, young women don't wait long enough to find out what the guy is about, and if he has a hidden agenda. You let yourself become an emotional mess because you have a romantic movie playing out in your mind about how everything is going to work. However, you don't know where his head is and he probably doesn't know where yours is. He can't participate in the creation of the imaginary scenario that you have put him in.

QQ4U (Quick Questions for You): How much do you really know about this guy? How do you know what you know about him? Are the details you have gathered from a reliable source? Do you know whether he already has a girlfriend? If you don't care about that, and want to be with him anyway because you believe that he will be better off with you, what does that say about you? Does he just want to add your name to his list of "accomplishments"? Does he believe in having only one girl in his life at a time? Some guys do, but many don't, because, collectively, many young women make it too easy for guys to have an assortment of young ladies to spend time with whenever they are ready.

Does this guy have goals that he's actively working toward accomplishing? Does he have any academic goals? Does he want to start his own business? Succeed in a line of work he knows something about? What vision does he have for his life?

Of course, there are plenty of successful people who had an underperforming academic record and then went on to success, but probably just as many had GPAs that were in the toilet and have gone nowhere. If he is planning to go to college, is it an accredited college or university to which he has actually applied, or has he been accepted to Basement U—his mama's basement? What proof is there that he is moving toward success? What is he actively doing that shows progress toward his goals? And, finally, is he so into himself that his ego is taking up all the room that would be available to a caring individual such as you?

If you are still in high school but you are into someone who is in college, do you realistically expect a relationship to blossom, or continue? It's not impossible, but experience says it's not likely. I was talking to a young lady one day who had met a guy while she was in high school, and he was ending his first year of college. My first thought was: "Are you serious? You mean to tell me that you think this guy, who is away at school, is going to have a serious, singular interest in a high school junior?" But, at that point, I simply said to her, "Wow...that's great!" It's not likely that she would have listened to sound logic about the situation, even if it made total sense. She was already in takeoff mode. I knew that it would be a matter of time before she realized that, with her, he was interested in only one thing, and that she was setting herself up to be just his weekend experience when he came home. He was probably spending time with someone else when he was away at school.

So, continuing the true story: Of course, this guy was "really cute," and he said that he wanted her number so that he could call her and get to know her. After several text messages, and a few conversations, he said that he was really "feelin' her," and wanted to get to know her better. She immediately had visions of what their future together could look like, even though he was miles away.

Well, the scenario played out for a few months. In the beginning, she was happy to see him whenever he came home, although he never invited her up to the campus on weekends. His excuse for this? He told her he had to stay at school because he had "so much homework," even though the pictures posted on his social media told a different story. After a while, she began asking when he was going to come home again because she missed him, and that she didn't like the fact that he never asked her to come up to visit him.

She began to demand more of his time and would constantly text him, but at this point he wasn't responding. Eventually, she found out that he had a girlfriend on campus. When she came to talk to me about it, she was distraught. She didn't understand what had happened and wanted to know what she had done wrong. This is when I had to get serious with her to help her see how she had put herself into that tough situation.

THINK ABOUT IT

What mistakes do you think she made?

Before she had a chance to assess whether this guy was really interested in her, she allowed herself to become a mess. First of all, most young men who are in college are not interested in a young lady who is still in high school, no matter what they may say. College is fresh and exciting; high school is back then. Second, if she hadn't become so excited about him and the possibilities of a "relationship" simply because he smiled at her, said that he was "feelin' her," and sent her a few text messages, she could have taken the time to really think about whether there was any potential for a real relationship. She could have logically thought out whether her dream made sense.

I mean ... really????

A recently graduated high school student came back to school to visit while he was home for winter break. Quickly, word spread throughout the school, particularly to one young lady who was still a student there and had really liked him before he went off to college. As soon as she found out that he was in the building, she found some of her friends and positioned herself to "coincidentally" bump into him. She and her friends made themselves very conspicuous so that he couldn't avoid seeing them. The young lady rolled her eyes at him while her friends were "getting her back" in the background. But no matter what she did to get his attention, he just looked at her and shook his head. She and her friends huffed and puffed as they walked away.

Once the girls had left, he told me that he had been interested in the young lady while he was STILL IN HIGH SCHOOL, but now that he's in college, he's looking to connect with a young woman with whom he has more in common. In other words, in college. He showed me her picture. This guy has integrity; he isn't the type to take advantage of a girl. However, if he had been the type to prey on someone's weaknesses, the young lady who obviously liked him would have made herself an easy target. She would have been *someone to do* if he was a different kind of guy.

You may be thinking that if he was that type of guy, the blame would fall on him. Sorry, but I disagree. IT'S TIME FOR A REALITY CHECK! He's away at college, so, HELLO!!!! He's going to be interested more seriously in someone he can see on a regular basis, not just on weekends or during school break.

A few years ago, there was a young man who was new to the school who immediately got the attention of several girls. OMG, the young ladies did everything to get him to notice them. They tried to sit next to him class. Between classes, they would hang out by his locker. They tried to sit with him in the cafeteria. After he had been there for a few weeks, they began to accidentally (ha!) bump into him, and joke with him excessively. They would do anything to get his attention.

One day I pulled him aside and suggested that he be careful not to send false signals to any of these young ladies. I told him that even though he was not pursuing any of them they obviously couldn't contain themselves whenever he was around. I asked him to be sure to pay close attention to how he interacted with them. He told me that his dad had told him the same thing, which reinforced the fact that my advice to him was sound. For a while, he really seemed to manage things, until...

He began dating a young lady in the school who was a sophomore while he was in his junior year. They were a cute couple and seemed to be into each other. They continued to date into his senior year, and his girlfriend was really into him. It's not that he wasn't into her, but she was beginning to lose it because he was moving toward graduation and preparing to go away to school. He took her to prom, and they continued to date until he went off to college. Predictably, once he had settled in there, his text messages and calls to her became inconsistent, and eventually stopped altogether. She couldn't handle it and became depressed to the point where she was missing school. Her grades slipped and she barely graduated on time. She didn't assess the situation, and as a result, really became a mess.

Assessing is an ongoing process. You don't make an assessment one time and then stop doing it because you are in a relationship. Because life changes from day to day, so do the dynamics of living.

You really have to pay attention to how circumstances evolve in every situation.

I have listened to several young women who actually believed they were in a relationship with a guy, only to discover that they were actually in a relationship with their own self-concepts or dreams. When you are the only one working to make a relationship work while he is sitting on the sidelines, you are in a YOUSHIP, not a relationship.

Recently, two different young ladies from two different schools asked for my opinion. Each of them was brokenhearted because they couldn't understand why the young men they liked seemed distant. In both cases, they were in a YOUSHIP, but didn't realize it.

"But, I love him …"

A young lady told me about what was happening in her "relationship" with her "boyfriend." She said that whenever they break up he would spend time with other females. When I asked her how often they spent time together, she told me that she saw him only about once a month. I asked her how often she heard from him, and she said that she only heard from him occasionally. So, I asked her: "What relationship are YOU in, because obviously he has checked out and has moved on to whatever, or whoever else." Her response was, "But I love him! I'm good for him. I can help him be a better person."

QQ4U: Why do so many young women feel compelled to help guys become better people? What makes this your responsibility? I'm just asking … but back to the story …

SMH. I just sat there and looked at her. After a few minutes had passed, I asked her to describe her ideal relationship. She gave me examples of how a relationship **should** look by explaining that it's when people communicate with each other, spend time with each other, go to the movies, trust each other, grow together, or whatever. Her answer was correct. Then I asked her if her "relationship" was even close to her definition of what one should look like.

Of course, she said "No, not really. But, it has the potential to be that way." And, again, she said, "But I love him." And again, *SMH*.

So let's process this situation together. A lot of young women—and older ones too—get so caught up in what they think is a relationship that they don't realize they are not even in one. Maybe in the beginning this guy was interested in her, but somewhere along the line, for whatever reason, he changed his mind and dropped out of it. Remember, **you need to slow your roll** long enough to be able to see whether you are together with him, or together with yourself. This young woman, like so many, was doing everything to make things work with someone who wasn't even there.

Let's look at another situation. I was near a young woman who began crying profusely for no apparent reason. A stream of huge tears flowed from her eyes. When I asked her what was wrong, she told me that she would tell me after class.

When she was ready to share what had triggered her emotional outburst, she told me that she had just found out that her "boyfriend" had been cheating on her. So I asked her some of my usual questions. This is how that conversation went:

"So, when is the last time you saw your boyfriend?"

RESPONSE: "I have only seen him a few times. We usually communicate by text messages."

"OK. When is the last time you heard from him?"

RESPONSE: "A few weeks ago."

"How long has this been going on?"

RESPONSE: "A few months."

SMH ... What makes you think he's your boyfriend?

RESPONSE: "He told me that he's really into me. I love him."

A lot of you just really want to be loved. You want someone to pay attention to you and make you feel special. It's natural for you to want to have someone special in your life. I get it. I really do. But you must apply some degree of logic and reasoning when it comes to dealing with a guy. You need to pay attention to his behavior, like what he is and isn't doing. And, just because things are not working out with him, that does not mean something is wrong with YOU! Remember that. I will come back to this a little later.

But the bottom line is this: A lot of young men are not ready for a relationship—at least not the type of relationship you have in mind. They may give you the impression they are interested in commitment, but many of them are not. Many of them are in-the-moment guys. They meant what they said when they said it. But, if the moment is too long, they check out and leave you standing there wondering what just happened.

Lesson 2

WIDE OPEN! KEEP YOUR EYES AND EARS OPEN

Several young men have admitted to me that when they are in a relationship, they often feel an enormous amount of pressure to be something they don't know how to be. When you begin to shift from liking him into acting like you want to be his "forever girl," it may cause you to have unreasonable expectations of someone who can't decide what he is going to want from one minute to the next.

One young man, 17, who was preparing to graduate from high school, had this to say: "It's not that we don't like our girlfriends, because we do. But they are so serious about everything. They have gone from being fun to acting like they own us or something.... They are always telling us what to do. They ask us a ton of questions about where we're going and what we're doing when we aren't with them. And, when we do tell them, all they do is ask us why we're doing whatever and complain. It's just too much work."

So, my advice to you is to go with the flow ... and don't be too intense. Remember, both of you are young. You have your entire life ahead of you to get serious.

Why did he change his mind about wanting to be with me?

Several young men have told me that when they decided to either end the relationship or just move on to whatever else, it's difficult for them because their girlfriends are not willing to accept how they feel. They have a hard time telling you the truth because they don't want to hurt your feelings. While they are trying to figure out the best way to end things between the two of you, many of you just keep insisting on "fixing" things between the two of you. You are not dealing with the reality that there is nothing to be done. It's over, and he wants out. And a lot of times it has absolutely nothing to do with you.

But maybe it does….

So, it may be time for a self-assessment. First, you are in the process of discovering yourself. You are trying to figure out who you are while your guy is trying to figure out who he is at the same time. This is not an easy life stage, and it can go on through most of your youth. But for guys, it seems to be different. Many of them are not thinking long term when it comes to a relationship. They are into things like sports, music, video games, and gym shoes. Oh, and they are into sex, but they don't always have a full grasp of intimacy. It's important that you understand the difference between intimacy and sex because it can drive the difference between how you and your young man view the relationship. Intimacy entails more of a commitment, but sex really does not.

I once had a conversation with a young man who was in his first year of college. He admitted that after he graduated from high school his priorities changed. He had to become more focused on what he needed to do to get his act together. When he was in high school, he was quite the ladies' man. In fact, at any given time he was involved with at least two girls at his school, which caused a lot of confusion. I can't say that it was entirely his fault because there was a competition between the girls to see who could be the one to "get him."

While I was talking to him, he and a young man who was still in high school began to reflect on their "player" days. They both spoke openly about the number of girls they had been with over the years and they both had the same attitudes. They said the girls they had sex with didn't mean anything to them. They said:

- Because the young ladies made themselves so available, the guys felt they had put themselves in that position to be used. "Well, do you think I am just going to say no?" one of them asked. "I mean, if you put it there like that what do you expect?"
- They never considered having a relationship with any of the young ladies involved.
- They had no plans to date or romance any of the young women involved because they weren't interested in that.

Meanwhile, the young ladies involved were more than willing to be as loving and supportive as they knew how. However, none of these young ladies had conducted a proper assessment. If they had they would have known that neither of these guys had any intention of settling on one girl. Why? They had so many options that they didn't have to.

Before you move too quickly with your feelings about someone without fully assessing, ask yourself how much your heart is worth to you.

Hookin' up via social media

Between Instagram and Snapchat and so on, you are given opportunities to connect with people like never before. I get that this is the norm for many of you. Just be careful. Remember, people only show you what they want you to see. If you are not skilled in the art of reading a person's body language or overlooking a statement a person may be making about his character based on the pictures he posts, you could be opening the door to having unhealthy interactions.

For example, let's say that a young man posts several pictures of himself partially clothed, perhaps without his shirt. What message is he conveying about himself? With him choosing that photo, what do you think his priority is in a relationship? Or, perhaps a young man posts pictures of himself in a compromising position with other young women. Maybe a young man will post pictures flashing money, or other items that will give the viewer the impression that he may have a lot going on. I am not judging, but I am asking you to use your assessment skills to think about who this guy may be in real life, or what he thinks is most important in hooking up. Is he simply seeking attention, or is he telling you part of his story through his pictures?

Don't be dismissive of what you see in a post and blow it off. Look at the pictures and read his comments. In fact, read the responses to what he has posted, and read his responses to the posts, which can also be insightful. Often, his response lets you know where his head is and what he's looking for.

Social media is one of the main sources for people of all ages to make connections, and I get it. Believe me, I do understand. But there is an old-school method where people would ask to *lay an eyeball* on someone. Back-in-the-day, grandparents and parents would expect a young woman to bring her gentleman of interest around them so they could see him and talk to him in person. I know this may sound extreme to you, because whenever you introduce someone to your family it immediately gives the impression that you and your guy must be pretty serious about each other.

Well, this is not always true. If you like someone, it is good to get feedback from those who love you and have your best interest at heart about whoever this person may be. It is very easy to overlook certain behaviors or character flaws when you are too close to the situation. When your friends and family are able to meet your guy, they can also observe how he interacts with you, talks to you, and whether he can hold his own with them. It doesn't have to be intense, but long enough for your observers to get their read on the situation.

Once they get their read, the rest is up to you. In other words, you have to keep an open mind. You have to keep an open heart. And you have to keep open ears. When someone you love and trust tells you what they think about the young man you're seeing, please listen. Pay attention now so you won't have regrets later.

For example, let's say you have met a young man, and you two have taken an interest in each other. While the two of you are still getting to know each other, you introduce him to one of your friends. As soon as you can, you call your friend to get her opinion. Here is how your conversation goes:

You: So, what do you think? Girl, isn't he cute?

Friend: Yeah, he seems OK.

You: OK? Is that all you have to say?

Friend: I mean, if you like him, I guess that's all that matters.

You: I really want you to tell me what you think about him. I know you, and I know you have my back. I really want to hear your thoughts.

Friend: Well, I didn't like it when he kept staring at me when you left the room to go into the kitchen to say hi to my mother. His conversation made me uncomfortable. He kept asking me what I like to do in my free time. I told him that I play tennis, and that I like sports. He told me that he really digs a young woman who is into sports. But as soon as you came back in the room, he changed the subject.

You: Girl, he talks to all my friends that way. You're making a big deal out of nothing.

Friend: Well you asked me to tell you what I think. So, that's what I have to say.

Of course, you are a bit upset with your friend's feedback, because she didn't say what you wanted to hear. And even though you trust her because she has always been there for you, you have a feeling that she is jealous of you and your new "bae," so you ignore what she has to say.

On another occasion, you introduce your guy to a cousin who is visiting from out of town. You two are close and have stayed connected via texts and social media. But you haven't seen her in a while, so you're really excited to be able to hang out with her and introduce her to your close friends, including the one who just "hated on" your new guy the other day. After your friends have met your cousin, and your guy, you ask your cousin what she thinks of him:

You: So, what do you think of him?

Cousin: Is that the guy you have been telling me about? I was expecting him to be different.

You: What do you mean?

Cousin: I don't know. He really doesn't seem to be your type. He doesn't seem like he is into you as much as you think.

You: What do you mean? We're together all the time! I can't keep him away from me!

Cousin: If you say so. I just kept checkin' out how he kept looking at your friends when your back was turned. I mean, he didn't do anything out of line, but he kept staring at them, especially when they walked by. He looked at me, too, but I gave him the "I don't think so" look, and he looked away. I think you can do better.

You: You're just mad because you and your boyfriend recently broke up. I know he's into me. I don't want to talk about this anymore.

OK, let's back up a minute. Two people you trust, and don't know each other, are telling you the same thing about this guy.

IF TWO OR MORE PEOPLE WHO DON'T KNOW EACH OTHER AND HAVE NEVER TALKED TO EACH OTHER ARE MAKING THE SAME COMMENTS, YOU NEED TO PAY ATTENTION TO WHAT EVERYONE IS SAYING!

There is something you are REFUSING to see in him. The signs are there, but you are too close to the situation to notice. This is why the old *laying an eyeball* technique is so valuable. It helps you to see the good, the bad, and the ugly.

The reality is that you don't need a relationship to be happy. You are whole and complete right where you are! You don't need to have someone in your life to validate you. I do understand that most of you really want meaningful companionship, which is natural. You just need to give thought to what you want in a guy, and why those things matter to you.

FOUR-WEEK ASSESSMENT TOOL

Perhaps you are well on your way to developing ways to pace yourself before you dive in too deeply and end up over your head. If so, good for you! You will save yourself a great deal of heartache by having safeguards in place. But if you're new to assessing, here is a week-by-week guide to help with your **slow-your-roll** process.

WEEK ONE
- Check out his social media profile. What impression does it leave you with?
- What types of pictures are posted? Do his images mirror what you believe to be appropriate?
- After meeting, who sends the first message (text, Instagram, etc.) after you meet? What does it say?
- How frequently does **he** initiate contact with you?

WEEK TWO
- What effort is he making to get to know you? Has he asked you about your interests or your goals? Does he have any himself?
- Has he talked to you about having sex? If you have spent time with him, has he attempted to become physical with you?
- How long does it take him to respond to your text messages?
- What are some of his values? Does he respect women? If so, how do you know?
- What are the main topics of his messages with you? Is there any depth? Is he suggesting that you do anything for him, like loan him money, pick him up, drop him off, etc.?
- Has he suggested that the two of you get together? Is he asking questions about when he can come by, and who will be at your house when he gets there?

- Has he asked you out on a date? Where has he asked you to go? How are you supposed to connect to see each other... will it be his responsibility, or yours?

WEEK THREE
- What do you know about him this week that you didn't know about him in weeks one and two?
- What are some more of his values?
- Has he talked to you about having sex?
- Has he attempted to touch you inappropriately?
- Has he asked you to send him explicit pictures? Has he sent any revealing pictures to you?
- Does he seem happy to hear from you?
- Why does he say he's interested in you?
- Is he placing any demands on you?
- What are some of his habits?
- When you two communicate, is there an equal outreach between the two of you?
- If you suggest getting together, what is his response? Does he have other plans?
- Does he show interest in those things that matter to you?
- How often does he say he'll get back with you, but never does?
- Does he frequently sound agitated when you suggest spending time with him?

WEEK FOUR
- How often does he reach out to you? When you contact him, does he respond right away?
- Does he seem busier now that he did when you first met?
- Does he seem happy to hear from you, or does he seem distant?
- Is he still showing interest in spending fun, quality time with you?

- How many times do you reach out to him before he responds?

If you use this four-week assessment tool as your guide before you open your heart to someone, you may discover that he may not be a good fit for you before you become emotionally invested.

The practice of asking the right questions

Whenever you are getting to know someone it's good to ask some questions that require more than a one-word response because an in-depth response can create an opportunity for conversation, offer insights, and lead to more questions. I am not suggesting that you interrogate a young man to the point that he feels you're badgering him. I'm simply suggesting that if you ask the right questions you might get responses that will let you know how much time you're willing to invest in getting to know someone.

For example, let's say you meet a young man and you want to get to know something about him. After the basic exchange of each other's names, you ask if he has a girlfriend.

He simply says, "No."

You stand there hoping he wants to know the same thing about you, and you assume that because he said he doesn't have a girlfriend he may be available. But nothing is happening. Perhaps you didn't ask the right question. What if you had asked, "How recently have you been in a relationship with someone?"

Well, that question could be a game changer! Because now there is potential for a response, such as, "I've been in an off-and-on relationship with someone for some time. We're not together at the moment, but we've been through this before. I really don't know what we're doing right now."

As you can see, asking a different type of question led you to knowing a whole lot more, including that although he doesn't consider this other young woman his girlfriend, they do have a history that is continuing to evolve.

At this point, you will have to decide what your next step will be. On one hand, any young woman who comes along at this point—such as you—may be only a distraction for him, and she may not be someone he would seriously consider. If you were listening to what he said, and how he said it, you might be able to figure that out and decide that he's not ready to let go emotionally. Not only that, if he doesn't ask you if you're involved with someone, he might not be interested in working to establish a relationship with someone new.

If you are in tune with your intuition and you get the feeling that it would be better to just let it go, you should listen to yourself because you are probably right. Remember, there will always be a chance to connect with someone else at another time.

On the other hand, you can take a chance and try to connect with him anyway, if you can get his attention. You can forget about the importance of asking the right questions because, as you begin chattering away, telling wayyyyyy too much of your business, you are not giving him a real opportunity to talk so you can LISTEN. In your moment of eagerness to get to know him, you forget to consider that you don't know with certainty whether the young lady he has been involved with has moved on. You may be putting yourself in the middle of a messy situation if she finds out about you and thinks you are trying to take her man. A scenario like this can lead to a lot of unnecessary drama!

If you stop to think and ask some questions that will let him open-up, they will provide the feedback you need before you go into emotional takeoff into the world of hopeful possibilities. Remember, you have **to slow your roll, and assess**, especially when you are first getting to know someone. Keep in mind that many young men are only going to answer the questions that are being asked. They will give you "yes" and "no" answers all day if that's the only response required.

Let's practice this technique together. Remember, one key to the effectiveness of this strategy is to be non-threatening. You simply want to ask questions so you can assess the situation. Here's a scenario:

You met a young man a few days ago, and it feels like you both want to get to know each other. You are moving along using the assessment tools presented earlier in this lesson to help you pay attention to his consistent attentiveness and interest. As you are ending week one of your "warm and fuzzy" period, he tells you that you are everything he has ever wanted in someone, and he can see you in his future.

That sounds great, doesn't it?!? But, wait—before you get excited about how he is so into you so quickly, don't you wonder how can he make that decision about you in such a short amount of time?

TALK ABOUT IT...

What are a few questions a young lady could ask him to determine where he is coming from, so she can decide whether to invest any more time in getting to know this guy better?

1.

2.

3.

4.

5.

Learning how to ask the right questions, and listening to the responses, is a skillful art that can help you navigate many situations in life. Even when the answers may not be what you may want to hear, wouldn't you rather have the information you need rather than having to guess, or never know? Practice asking the right types of questions. You will save yourself headaches—and heartaches—when you do.

Why do you like me?

As you are refining your ability to ask questions, I have another question for you to add to your arsenal. Some of you may already ask this question when a guy says he likes you. Do you ever ask him why he likes you? If not, you should make it a habit. Why?

His response can be very revealing. Whatever he tells you, pay close attention. Consider what he *says* he likes about you, and how he engages you based on the reason(s) he offers. And, it's important that you ask him this question *face-to-face*. Why?

Because you need to be able to read his body language when he responds. Does he look directly at you when he answers, or does he look away? Does he have to stop and think about his answer, or does it easily roll of the end of his tongue?

Finally, do you really believe him? What are your instincts telling you about how he answers? If you have trust issues yourself, no matter what he says, you may doubt him. But if you are able to listen and pay attention to how he says what he says, you may be able to determine the degree of sincerity of his answer. On the other hand, if you believe everything he says because *you love him*, you may need to develop some additional skills of discernment to keep you from being played over and over again.

For example, let's say you meet a young man at a party at the home of a mutual friend. Your friend thinks the two of you would make a cute couple, and she encourages you both to get to know each other. You two exchange numbers, and he begins texting you and reaching out to you on Instagram. You begin your assessment process by checking out his social media, which appears to be totally appropriate. He has posted pictures with his family and friends having a great time at concerts and sports events. Some of his posts are inspirational quotes made by famous people. One post makes reference to the importance of participating in community service. Based on your observations, he seems to have a great deal of potential! But of course, you need to give things more time. ...

It's still early in the game, but the two of you seem to be hitting it off. You let him know that you share his interest in music and sports. He says that you're *dope* and that he really likes that in a young woman. He adds that he has more in common with you than anyone he's met. He seems to enjoy talking to you, although most of your conversations are brief. He sends you thoughtful text messages telling you that he really likes you, and you tell him that you like him, too.

He has taken you to the movies a few times, which is nice, but he has never invited you to go with him to any of the sports events he goes to even though he knows you are into sports. Whenever you mention that you would like to go to a game with him, he tells you that he usually goes with his "boys." Later, you inquire about some of his community projects and you ask to get involved with the same organization. But he doesn't make it happen. No matter what you suggest, he always seems to have a reason not to include you in activities where you two have common interests. He is not connecting with the very part of you that he claims is attractive to him.

When a guy says he really likes you, what you're about and what you're in to, but he's not engaging the part of your personality that he says he admires, you should be curious enough to want to know what's going on. That's why the "why do you like me" question should be asked in person. You get to see the body language along with his response. I am not suggesting that you question him with an attitude and a neck roll. You just want to know what liking you means to him.

And be prepared for whatever his answer may be. Don't accept "I don't know why, I just do" as an answer because it's vague and doesn't reveal anything. Remember, this is part of your new strategy of asking the types of questions that will help you open your eyes and keep them open about the person you are dealing with, and *how he is dealing with you.* If he never invites you to a game or to watch one on television, what's up with that?

It could be that he likes some things about you, but does not necessarily see you as part of his vision for a relationship. Sometimes people are attracted to certain features that a person has and may not necessarily have an interest in establishing something meaningful with that person. Sometimes the mixed messages that a guy sends may be totally innocent.

Lights, video, ACTION!!!

One of the best ways to assess someone is to observe them in a variety of settings. If you always see a person under the same circumstances, you don't get a clear picture of who they really are. How can you know who you're dealing with if you only see one aspect of his personality?

I know a couple who attend school together and spend all their time with each other in school. They never get together on weekends to go to the movies or games, or out to eat. When I asked the young man why he never took his girlfriend out, he said he had never really thought about it. **SMH!** How can his girlfriend know who he really is, or how can he know who she really is, if neither of them has seen each other operating in a different environment?

When you don't spend time with your guy around his friends, your friends, or out in public, it is impossible to get to know the *real* person. It's easy for someone to show you only what they want you to see when you can't observe them in a variety of settings. You need the lights on, and the video rolling, to see the honesty of their actions and to find out if there is another part of their personality they might be hiding. You need to see how they behave in a variety of settings, and how they react to different people and circumstances, and how people react or respond to them.

So, if you want to get a real screen-shot of who your guy is, broaden your horizons. If he never wants to go anywhere with you and restricts his relationship with you to one kind of space, you are dealing with only part of a person. You will never know if he is truly worthy of you.

Love vs. Like

The question "Why do you like me?" should be asked periodically when you're in a relationship with someone because it's a way of checking in with each other. Even though you may have been dating for a while, it's good to stay connected to those things that brought the two of you together in the beginning (quite frankly, a guy who is really in tune with you should be asking you why you like him as well). It's good to be reminded of why you are still in a relationship because sometimes people stay together out of habit, not because the "like" is still there.

I knew a couple who had been dating for a long time. They were still cute together, but there was obvious distance between. Whenever someone asked him about her, or asked her about him, they each identified themselves as being in a relationship with each other. Yet whenever they were in the same space, they seemed to be worlds apart.

Here's another scenario: A young lady had the feeling that her boyfriend didn't like her anymore; they were always arguing, and one of them was always complaining about what the other was doing. She said they loved each other, but didn't seem to like each other. In spite of this, he was there whenever she really needed him. But after the need was met, the distance between them would return. For instance, someone made a very unkind remark about this young lady in a group text. It was the typical hater drama, for whatever reason, and before long, it was all over social media. When her boyfriend found out about it, he stepped in to protect her and advised the "haters" who were bullying her to "fall back" from any more drama. She was grateful that he was there for her. For a while, they started laughing, talking, and acting just as loving to one another as they were when they first met. But after a few days, they returned to their habit of arguing and getting on each other's nerves.

There should be a discussion about why they like each other, and the difference between "like" and "love." In an ideal situation, both emotions are present. But this is not always the case. Love is a much deeper emotion which involves genuinely wanting the best for the other person. You want them to be happy and successful, even if you are not around to share their significant experiences with them. Liking someone helps you to genuinely enjoy another person's company. You feel good when you are with them. You want to experience a variety of activities with them. You like talking to them, and you enjoy listening to them. You can love someone, but there are bound to be times when you don't necessarily like them. You can love someone, and not necessarily choose to go out of your way to spend time around them. Simultaneously liking and loving someone is a key ingredient in the formula that makes relationships work.

So, periodically tell your guy why you like him, and remember to ask him why he likes you. That's how you keep your finger on the pulse of your relationship.

What's his line?

Sometimes young men are creative in their introduction because they want to impress you. Sometimes a guy will run a line on you because he knows you think he's cute. Sadly, you are so busy looking at him and thinking about how great you would look together as a couple that YOU DON'T EVEN KNOW HIS LAST NAME. You aren't even listening to what he is saying to you!

What are some of the things guys say? I asked a few young men to share some of the lines they use. These young men were very candid and explained that it is not uncommon for guys to try to get their way by playing the victim. Here are some of their most effective go-to lines:

- "I have been through a lot, and I have trust issues."
- "I don't have anyone to support me."
- "You don't understand how difficult it is when everyone looks down on you without knowing anything about you."

Now, in some instances, guys who say these things may be sincere in their expressions. You are not going to know whether they are being real with you unless you **slow your roll**, take your time to **assess** them on many levels, and keep your eyes open and your mouth closed (unless you're asking a useful question). You don't have to let them know you're in observation mode. If you are patient, the truth you are seeking will be revealed.

A line for now, a line for later...

What you need to know about guys and their lines is that they don't only use them when they first meet you. They may also use them while you are dating, either to hold your attention or to keep you hooked while other things are going on behind your back!

For example, I knew of a young couple who had been dating for quite some time. They were both very bright, but she was more focused on setting and reaching her goals than he was. She did everything to encourage him (as many of you do), but he just wasn't there yet with his planning. In spite of this, he would always tell everyone that "she is my future wife and the mother of my kids." He would say this to her, and everyone who would listen. Whenever anyone heard him say this, especially another young woman, their immediate response was "awwwwwwww, that's so sweet!" It sounded so loving, right? Of course it did. It sounded loving to her—and to the other young lady he was running the same line on behind her back.

Lesson 3

YOU DON'T HAVE TO TWERK IT TO WORK IT!

It isn't healthy to link your self-worth to whether a guy wants you or not. And do not sell yourself short by using sex to get and hold on to a guy. As one young man told me, love does not mean:

Legs
Open
Very
Easily

There is no love in giving yourself to someone who doesn't deserve you or someone you are using sex to control or keep. This seems to be a big problem for young women who struggle with low self-esteem or self-image. You want to be loved, and your feelings bubble up and pour out. Sometimes you are bubbling over with so much love that you unintentionally impose your feelings and demands on someone else who may not feel the same way.

You don't have to twerk it to work it! You don't have to resort to using your body to capture a guy's heart. Just think about it ... if you do this with every guy you meet, hoping that he's "the one"—every time you move too quickly before you assess, don't read the signs, or don't wait long enough to know who this guy is—you could be setting yourself up for a revolving door of guys in and out of your life. Once you create this type of serial relationship cycle, the pattern can be hard to break.

Using sex to manipulate a young man into wanting to be with you is a risky strategy because there is a high probability that it will backfire. Not only can the guy treat you like less than the person you are, there can be unwelcome complications such as pregnancy and sexually transmitted disease. You can victimize yourself.

I've heard far too many heartbreak stories involving sex. Far too many young women have shared their stories of unsuccessful intimacy with me. Some of you have convinced yourselves that having sex with a young man is a necessity if you intend to "lock him down," because you believe that your ability to entice him is like signing a contract that will seal the deal. Countless women—young and old—have tried to use this technique as a means of getting a man and securing a relationship. But think about it: If a countless number of women are using sex to get a guy, doesn't that create countless opportunities for guys to have sex with multiple women?

You may have convinced yourself that sharing your body is not a big deal, and that I'm the one who is trippin' for even bringing it up. I can tell you that your journey dealing with young men is just beginning. I remember a young woman who was really into athletes; each guy she had an interest in was always on the football or basketball team. She was especially into the football team's captain for many reasons, starting with these two: He was a good-looking guy and she was the envy of all of the other young women because she was with him. An added perk was that everyone knew she was the captain's girl, which allowed her to command a certain level of respect at school. She also knew that he could be with anyone he wanted, and for that reason she needed to work hard to keep him. So she made sure she did everything she needed to do to keep his interest. She thought that if she did whatever he demanded, he wouldn't give any thought to the other young women who were flirting with him and making it known that they were available.

You won't be surprised when I tell you that she wasn't the only one he was in with. When she found out, she was heartbroken. To get back at him, she had sex with another guy, which led to the two of them breaking up.

But there was a really cute basketball player who had been checking her out for some time and was first in line to get next to her when her relationship had ended. He seemed genuinely concerned about her, but she explained that she wanted him only as a friend for the time being.

Before long their friendship deepened, and she believed that he was really the one she wanted. They became intimate. Then she found herself repeating the same mistakes. To keep him from straying, she gave more and more of herself to him. She thought she had him hooked. And she did for a while. But one day he ran into his ex-girlfriend and realized he had never really gotten over her. Suddenly, the young lady who was doing all she could to make things work discovered that things weren't working out after all. The basketball player she loved eventually told her he wanted to give his ex another chance. Again, she was left with a broken heart.

Her list of heartbreaks grew right along with her sex life. At a young age, she'd already had sex with several young men. Each time the situation made sense to her. After all, each time he was "the one." Within a few years she had the reputation of being "that girl."

In another situation, a young woman who used sex as part of her strategy to sustain her relationships didn't really care about the number of guys she had been intimate with. She believed that having sex was the necessary norm; if you're with a guy, that's just what you do. It didn't seem to matter to her that she had given herself to several guys in less than two years. As far as she was concerned, if she kept trying long enough, eventually she would get it right with the right guy, and none of her failed attempts from the past would matter.

Several years later, while attending college, she met a great guy who seemed to have all of the qualities she had been searching for. On top of that, he made it clear that he was really into her.

Their relationship turned serious almost overnight. The young man decided that she would be his forever girl, and posted pictures of her on Instagram.

The congratulatory comments began pouring in, including from someone who had dated this young woman their senior year in high school. In his comment, he mentioned that he wished he "could have some of that again." His post led to several other guys posting similar comments. There were even some remarks that she would have been the marrying type if she hadn't been so used up.

The young college man was so dismayed by all of the comments that he confronted his girlfriend. She reminded him that she had told him that she had dated a few guys in the past, but things just never worked out. She went on to explain that she finally knew what real love was, and that she would never do anything to betray him. But he wasn't sure he could get past all that he was reading. Just as she had been looking for the right guy, he had been searching for the young woman who was right for him. He was confused, and didn't know what to do.

THINK ABOUT IT...

What should he have done about his relationship with the love of his life?

Whatever your solution for this couple may be, remember, it can be easy to solve someone's problem when you are not directly involved. In the age of social media, it is easier than ever for information to be circulated on a wide scale. And, as we will discuss in a later lesson, whenever you post anything on any social media, it is permanent; it never goes away.

If you're thinking about engaging in this behavior, and you become intimate every time you like a young man, there will be pieces of yourself floating around everywhere. Any mention of your history on social media may follow you for years to come.

Body count

Many of you probably know what this means. Body count refers to the number of people you've had sex with. Many guys tout their body count like it's a badge of accomplishment; the higher the count, the more "game" a young man has, and the more he is respected among his "bros." You may not care about how many times you lay down with different guys. Or you may believe that you have a sense of entitlement because you have had sex with them. But if they are on a mission to keep building their body count you will be only one thing to them: a number.

One day, when I found myself inadvertently *ear-hustling*, I overheard a group of guys talking about women. Even though a few had girlfriends and others didn't, they were all bragging about the number of women they had been with. Now, I know that there are some guys who exaggerate when they are with their "bros," because they don't want to sound inexperienced. But I knew these guys, and a few of them were discussing their actual experiences, and were talking in terms of real numbers.

The conversation they were having that day was not new to me because I had actually talked with a few of them about their involvement with young women before. And they made it clear that they had manipulated "some" of these young ladies and had taken advantage of their innocence by leading them to believe they were their "one and only." However, they insisted that there were many young women who just threw themselves at them. Unfortunately, they were telling the truth. How do I know? I have seen young women making it obvious that they were anxious, eager, and ready to get together with these guys.

Why would any young woman allow herself to be reduced to being nothing more than a number in a guy's body count? It seems that some young women like to be able to brag, themselves, about having had sex with a particular guy who was desired by a lot of young women, even knowing their chances of staying with him may have been highly unlikely. I guess they thought that having a piece of him for a moment was better than having nothing from him at all. *SMH*.

Now, there are some young men who do not base their interest in a young lady on whether she is willing to "give it up." Some have found that it was the young ladies who were "pushing up" on them! And, like most guys, they didn't say no. If a strong offer was being made, they took it, even if they had no deep interest in the young lady who was making the offer.

I had a set of separate conversations with a young man and his girlfriend about their unstable relationship. She would talk to me about their issues one day, and a few days later he would come to me with his side of the story. People who knew this couple were really getting tired of the daily drama that was occurring between them, most of which was coming from her. As I listened to him describe all the episodes, I made a bold move and directly asked him if the two of them were intimate. His response surprised me because while he said yes, he added that she was the one who had initiated sex. Since it was offered, he said he wasn't going to say no. He added that "I wasn't really pressed about it at the time, but she kept pushing up on me, so, why wouldn't I?" Because I knew the young lady he was involved with—and her obsession with him—I believed him. As many of you would say, she was always "doing too much."

What guys have to say about body count

It's interesting to have discussions with guys about body count because their attitude toward this depends on what their intentions are when it comes to dealing with young women. Young men who value **themselves** and understand the importance of valuing a potential girlfriend are concerned about how much random physical contact they have and are highly selective when it comes to sharing themselves with young women. They are deliberately seeking a supportive, stable relationship with a young woman who may have the potential to last long term, and even try to envision marriage.

Although many of these young men were raised without fathers, their mothers, grandmothers, and other significant women taught them to have a healthy admiration and respect for women. In fact, because of pain the meaningful women in their lives have endured, they are determined to not be like those men who were the source of that pain. These guys are also aware that in comparison to many young men they are more the exception than the norm.

Many young men are not thinking long term about a relationship because they don't have to. They are getting what they want without putting forth much effort! There are so many young women who give them undeserved access that they have no difficulty adding numbers, which works for them because it's all that matters to them anyway. So, unless your body counts **to you**, you may find yourself part of someone else's "count."

Body count, in reverse

In conversations with young men about body count, I found that some of them focused the discussion on the number of guys a young woman may have had sex with—*her* body count. They shared with me that when they like someone, they mention the young woman's name to a few of their friends to find out what they may know about her. If her name comes up in a certain way, she is immediately given the THOT label, and is put into the category of only being good for one thing.

I try to explain to them that, sometimes, if young women are searching for love in all the wrong places, perhaps some of their involvement with multiple young men may be a result of a sense of loneliness, of abandonment by father, or a strong need to be loved. The guys said that if a young woman "gets around," the psychology behind her behavior wouldn't matter. In other words, they are only tracking the body count, and not getting caught up with the story behind the numbers. So, be mindful of your own body count, because the word may travel faster than you could ever imagine.

This could be you ... in the future

Perhaps you know a more mature woman who has been lonely and miserable for years. No matter how hard such women try, they never seem to get it right with men. This pattern of unsuccessful relationships may well have begun when they were much younger, perhaps around your age. They may have been trying to "twerk it to work it," and allowed themselves to become part of too many different men's body counts. They have been used, and used up. Sometimes, angry, bitter women with unhealthy relationship patterns have such bad attitudes they inadvertently influence their daughters to have bad attitudes as well. I have known several young women whose behaviors I have been curious about until I met their mothers. At that point, I simply say to myself, "Oh ... I see where that comes from." No judgment, just an observation.

Don't allow yourself to become an angry, bitter young woman. If you are not mindful of this it may become part of your personality. You may become so difficult to deal with or so needy that no guy—and eventually, no man—will ever be able to satisfy your demands.

Remember, you don't have to twerk it to work it.

Lesson 4

LEVEL UP! WHAT LEVEL ARE YOU ON?

Frequently, when a young lady meets a young man, she tends to immediately put him into one of two categories: Level 1—he has potential for a relationship, or Level 2—he doesn't. Young men flip the process. Theirs are Level 1, she will, or Level 2, she won't. If you are easy to read, most young men can determine this right away. If the young man is looking for a steady relationship, meets you and decides you're a Level 1, your designation can cause you to literally become a lay-over until he moves on to the next opportunity. Or, if the guy is the thoughtful type, he won't even attempt to connect with you at his Level 1 because the opportunity you are creating is not what he wants.

So, if you are thinking long-term, in your eyes you want him to be Level 1 and you want him to be thinking you are his Level 2—and worth spending time with. Got it? OK, now let's consider that many young men in high school and college have a variety of sub-categories that help them determine how to invest their time. Here are some:

- Too Much Work/Attention-Seeking Girl—These are young women who constantly need attention, including those who have "daddy issues," tell too much of their business, have the potential to be disloyal, and will even cheat on a guy with one of his friends.

- Pretentious Girl—These young women put on airs, pretend they are something they are not and try to impress others by showing off their possessions.
- Passive Girl—These girls don't want to contribute to the relationship yet want the relationship to work.
- Perfect Girl—This is the young woman who is willing to work toward her own happiness, which young men find attractive. She is also understanding, outgoing, and spontaneous, and believes in the importance of a balanced relationship where both people are giving 100% to make things work.

Why should a guy's categories matter to you? While you are trying to make a decision about a guy—and, sometimes, mentally force a guy into your Level 1 or quickly dismiss him because he won't make the cut—your potential guy has begun the process of deciding in which category he's going to place you. Because young men work at a slower, more deliberate pace, they can take their time processing who you are and what your role will be in their world. They know that you are totally distracted by whatever ideas are dancing around in your head about a potential relationship, based on limited information. They are making decisions about whether you will be short-term or long-term. And they are deciding how long it will take (you know what I mean) or how long they are willing to wait.

Of course, there are some exceptions

Some young men mature well before adulthood. They think long-term and imagine what type of woman they want for their future. These are the young men who put place mental checkmarks next to your name as they make observations about how strong you are in their category with the most preferences. The thing of it is, they are not telling you that they're doing it. And, for these guys, the depth of your thinking, and your hopes, dreams and goals, can easily be determined through the quality of your conversation.

What guys say about their categories

It seems that guys all have clearly self-defined categories for young women, which allow them to decide what type of strategy to employ. Young men I have talked with who are in high school, their late teens and early twenties shared examples of how they make assessments about a young woman, such as:

- A dummy-down girl: a young lady who is only able to engage in conversations with limited topics, and who is too needy, for whatever reason.
- A "fun" girl: a young lady who is kept around strictly for entertainment purposes.
- A serious girl: a young woman with the potential for building a relationship.

So, guys in general are strategic about how they approach life. Many of them just want to get to the point of whatever matters, using as few words as possible. Have you ever sent a long text to a guy to ask a question, explain something, discuss plans, or share information? You really give a lot of thought to your text message before sending it to him, right? And how does he usually respond? By saying "OK." So, while you are chattering on about whatever you think is important, guys are strategically listening to you to determine which category to place you in.

The truth of the matter, as I mentioned in an earlier lesson about asking the right questions, is that many young women talk waaaaayyy too much! While you are chattering on trying to impress him, he may be listening to your conversation to hear where your head is, and what your priorities are. He can hear whether you are confident, or desperate. He can tell whether you are grounded, or flighty. He can tell whether you are real, or fake. It's amazing what you reveal about yourself every time you talk.

I'm not discouraging you from talking or making you afraid to say anything. I am encouraging you to LISTEN as well. When you're doing all the talking all the time, what are you learning about him? Where is his head? What is he thinking? What does he want?

Listen to what the guy has to say. Does he talk about his family? Does he talk about his dreams? Does he talk about sports? Does he talk about himself? DOES HE TALK ABOUT HIMSELF ALL THE TIME and not ask you questions to get to know who you are? It will be difficult for you to discern any of these things if you don't close your mouth and open your ears.

Remember, while he's talking, you are **assessing**. You are assessing to hear anything that will let you know whether he has the potential to be the right fit for you. You're also reading him to see—based on his conversation AND BODY LANGUAGE—whether you may be a good fit for him.

As I said earlier, you and most guys are in the process of figuring out who you are. And while you are in this early phase of self-discovery it is not only important for you to figure out what you want, it's just as important to try to identify what you don't want. If you begin to figure out what will not work for you, you can avoid spending a lot of time trying to make something work with someone who is not a good fit. Learning this lesson early will save you a lot of time and heartache as you progress through your life.

Lesson 5

BEING TOO NEEDY CAN MAKE YOU SEEM GREEDY

OK. This is a subject that you may not want to deal with, but it is difficult to discuss dating and relationships without addressing it. Give some real open-minded thought about whether this lesson applies to you.

You may be someone who really needs a lot of attention. You constantly need to be acknowledged. You constantly need to be told that you're special. You need to hear that you're desirable. You need to be told that you are loved.... ALL THE TIME! As the dictionary would say, you "have an intense and selfish desire for something."

Your neediness drives you to demand a young man's attention. You are uncomfortable when his focus is anywhere but on you. You would like to limit the time that he spends with his friends, and sometimes his family. You question him when he wants to do anything that doesn't include you. You constantly text him, and when he doesn't respond as quickly as you want you get an attitude. Then, when you're really frustrated, you turn to social media and publicly blast him. (This is a real no-no!) Your neediness has spiraled out of control. The bottom line is that when you become too needy, it can drive guys, and people in general, away from you.

What guys say about needy young women

Several guys had quite a bit to say on this subject. First, they would really appreciate it if you would be sensitive to some of the things that matter to them, and not always be focused on what matters to you. They say that many of you are looking for guys who are trying to get themselves together, yet, when they are doing the things necessary to make progress in their lives so they can be better men, you place time demands on them that are not fair or realistic. They can't spend all their time with you and work or attend to critical family matters at the same time.

In other instances, there are times when they want to engage in activities without you. There is nothing wrong with a young man enjoying some "guy time" with his friends. The sad reality is that many of you don't seem to care about the guy's needs. It doesn't matter if he wants to hang out friends or handle an emergency, your ego is screaming "Me! Me! Me!"

A few young men I have talked to expressed considerable frustration about experiences with girlfriends who simply didn't appreciate them. For example, they said that money they earn from their jobs is used to cover their personal expenses and contribute to their households, but you are so focused on yourself that you don't give any consideration to their priorities. They are trying to deal with their needs while you are complaining about how they are not doing enough for YOU!

They are not obligated to offer financial assistance, but some of you pressure them to make them feel guilty. When you do that, it makes them feel like you're using them. Some of them are fed up with your needy behavior while they are trying to get their own lives together. So if you don't show more understanding and willingness to see what's going on outside yourself, they may go looking for someone who is more considerate.

Guys I talked with complained that some of you have a strong sense of entitlement. For whatever reason, you seem to think that you are supposed to get your way simply because you are of the female persuasion. Take a moment to do a self-check. Do you think that everything is "all about you" because you are attractive? Or because you're young? Or because you're a woman? Don't you think you have to put forth effort to be the right type of person for yourself, first, and then be a quality person so you can attract a quality person? Give this some thought. It's not all about you, boo.

Several young men have told me about the number of young women who have, as they call them, "daddy issues." The guys are sensitive to this, but they find the needs of these young ladies are so overwhelming that they don't know what to do. So, they check out.

I recently observed the behavior of a young woman who was, as you would say, "being extra." She was so over the top I thought for a moment that I was watching a movie. When she walked into the room talking on her cell phone she was so loud that everyone there could hear her conversation. When she saw someone she knew, she made a point of letting everyone around her know that she knew this person. Her laughter was so loud that some people actually had to move away from where she was standing. Once she decided where she was going to sit, she kept getting up and walking around to call attention to herself. She had no idea that people were shaking their heads and rolling their eyes. Now, she was attractive and well dressed, but it was really an unfortunate scene. For whatever reason she needed so much attention she was willing to embarrass herself to get it.

In another situation, I talked to a young lady about her obvious constant need to have all eyes on her. To make that happen, she created chaos everywhere she went. She was super-dramatic and acted clueless, even though she really was smart. If people were engaged in a conversation, she would barge in and interrupt to ask a question that had nothing to do with whatever they were talking about. Before they knew it, she had hijacked their conversation, causing them to forget what they were talking about in the first place. So, because everyone considered her to be an air-head, they would simply dismiss her.

If she saw a guy looking in her direction, her behavior went into overdrive. Even when a guy really liked her and showered her with attention, it was never enough. She looked like a model—slender, statuesque, lovely facial features and a beautiful smile. But her antics were so annoying that people would stop talking whenever they saw her walking their direction. Or they would appear to be busy on their cell phones, just to avoid talking to her. As for the guy who liked her, I eventually found out that she wasn't the only fish he was trying to hook on his line.

Pay attention to how you are being driven by your emotional needs. Some of you may need counseling to help you work through your feelings of emptiness. You need to find a healthy way to address your issues. If you don't confront and deal with the deficiencies in your life, you might be setting yourself up for one unsatisfying relationship after another. You are not always the cause of your neediness, so don't just blame yourself. If you have a great dad and your neediness has nothing to do with family drama, there's another explanation for your emotional void.

Whatever the problem, you cannot expect your guy to fix it. For many young men, it's more than they can handle. You need to find someone wise and objective to help you understand your needs.

Am I too needy?

Before you begin this self-assessment, let me say that one of the most difficult things to do in life is to be totally honest with yourself. Being honest with yourself means that you should give yourself a fist-bump when you have gotten something right. However, it also means that you need to, when necessary, "check yourself before you wreck yourself" and make adjustments to your attitude, or some aspect of your personality. If you are needy, it would be wise to recognize it and deal with it before you drive your guy away. So, ask yourself, am I too needy?

Here is the deal with being needy. You are probably needy if:

- You dominate conversations because you need to be at the center of the action.
- You need your guy to constantly acknowledge you, especially when you are together around others.

- You complain if your guy has plans that don't include you, or he doesn't tell you everything he's doing.
- Whenever you talk to your friends, your boyfriend is the main subject of your conversation.
- You feel the need to let people far and wide know that you have a boyfriend and that he's really into you.
- You become emotional with him when you can't have your way.
- You place unreasonable demands on your guy's time.
- If someone tells you that you are too needy, you immediately argue with them. Of course, if you make a huge demonstration about the fact that you are not needy, you are probably needy.

If you can honestly admit to doing three or more of the above, sorry, but yes, you are needy. The question to ask yourself is, why? Perhaps you can begin your exploration of this question in Lesson 8, *He's Not Your Daddy and You Are Not His Mama!*

Lesson 6

HOW *YOU* MAKE A PLAYER

A young lady I knew was among several young ladies who liked the same guy at the same time. But no one liked this guy as much as he liked himself. Of course, he knew he was in demand and took full advantage of his position. He was so self-confident that he let all the young ladies who liked him know about each other. One of them was determined that she was going to be his one and only, and proceeded to tell the others that they needed to "fall back." Before long several young women were on the brink of fighting each other over a guy who wasn't really interested in any of them. SMH.

When you don't have clear expectations, and you have not decided what you will and will not tolerate, you make yourself a target for guys who don't have to put forth much effort to get you, and keep you. If every young lady insisted on being treated with respect, a lot of guys would rise to the occasion. A lot of guys wouldn't be players because they wouldn't have anyone to play with! You have to refuse to make things so easy for them ... you really deserve better.

So now you're thinking, "But what if he walks away and moves on to someone else?" Well, if he does, he's not into you anyway, so why should you waste your time? A lot of guys know they are playing a numbers game. They know that for every girl who feels good about her expectations, there are a lot of other girls who expect little or next to nothing. So, why should they step up their game for you when there are dozens of other young women who just want to have a boyfriend, even if they are constantly being played and cheated on?

I have known young men who were really nice guys—the kind any mother would want her daughter to date. But some fell into bad ways, caught by young women who would do almost anything to be with them. These guys became lazy about their own standards and expectations.

Most young women come to realize that they want to be with solid young men who are of great character and have strong values. There are a lot of nice guys who would like to date a nice young lady, and be able to call her his girlfriend (listen to me clearly ... I said DATE not MARRY. At this point, you should be more focused on how you are going to build a life for yourself, and not trying build your life around someone else). My point is that even the nicest guys can be corrupted by young women who do all the chasing.

Not all guys set out to be players. There are some great guys out there. And, you know may know this kind of guy, but you often view him as "just a friend" because he is so nice. This is your go-to guy. If you need a favor, he's there. He listens to you when your heart has been broken and gives you advice. But these guys often get overlooked because, according to many of you, they are TOO nice. This is really funny because these are the kinds of guys who actually have many of the traits you're looking for. But sometimes because their packaging is a bit off, they are too short, too tall, or too whatever, you won't give them serious consideration. You will use them, however, never giving any thought that doing this—or taking them for granted—is EXACTLY the type of mistreatment you have experienced that may have broken your heart. A wise saying very directly gets to this point by explaining that "Whatever you put out there will come back to you."

Now, in another situation, there were two young women who were trying to get the attention of the same young man, but he wasn't the type of guy who ordinarily received attention. He was a caring young man who may have been considered a bit ordinary, or perhaps even a nerd. Suddenly, he was the focus of the affection of not one but two young women at the same time. The young ladies, who had not had difficulty getting along with each other before, were suddenly embroiled in some serious drama. One posted nasty comments about the other, which caused a steady stream of heated insults to flow between them.

TALK ABOUT IT...

What do you think this guy should do about the situation?
Here's an old-school thought ... let a guy pursue you!

So, what does a chase look like?
The chase seems to be becoming a lost art because so many of you don't give a guy a chance to "step to you correctly" and show you that he is interested in **you**. When I say "chase" I am not suggesting that you become so difficult for a guy to pursue that he loses interest. And you don't want to be thought of as the kind of young lady who only plays games. What I am suggesting is that you let him take the steps to show that he is interested in you. Men are hunters by nature. They thrive on the pursuit. So, let him take some initiative ... let him "hit you up" with his text messages, and then you respond. You can reach out to him sometimes, but allow him the opportunity to plan a date, invite you out, and treat you like the lady that you are.

What guys have to say about chasing vs. being chased
The young men I have talked to about chasing vs. being chased said that they don't mind a young lady letting them know she's interested. Many of them said they won't even look your way if they don't think you'll be receptive. However, they were quick to add that they quickly lose interest when you go from letting them know that you are receptive to soaking up their space and not giving them any room to breathe. So, it's OK to be open, or perhaps take a

small first step toward a guy to let him know that you like him. But then fall back and let him make the next move. If he doesn't take the next steps, consistently, you should probably assume that he's not ready to move forward.

You've been iced!

Sometimes a guy may really like you but he is not ready to make a commitment. He admires you, and may even deeply like you and, perhaps, even loves you. But the notion of being with only one young lady at a time is too much for him to wrap his head around. Where you are concerned, however, he wants the best of both worlds. He wants to have the freedom to roam while he hopes you will wait for him to come back around. If you allow a guy to do this to you, you're being **iced.** In some instances, young ladies agree to being put on hold. However, a lot of times they may be clueless that they are being stored in the freezer until their guy takes them out to thaw.

Let's look at a situation where a young lady is **iced**. It seems as though the guy is really into her, that she is his #1. He constantly tells her how beautiful she is and that he admires her strength and determination, and appreciates how she always has his back. He tells her he knows she is going to be successful, and that he wants only the best for her. As they pursue their life interests, he insists that she is the one he can see himself with in the future and that she is definitely "wife material." Now that she is then convinced that she is the one for him, he asks her to wait for him until he is ready to settle down. He insists that he cannot imagine her with anyone else but him and that he would lose his mind if she spent time with anyone else.

The young lady feels special. She has her dream guy actually telling her everything she wants to hear. The fact that she has heard him tell other guys that she is his, and is "off the market," gives her a sense of security. And because good guys seem to be hard to find she thinks it would be foolish not to take everything he has said to her to heart. What if she doesn't wait, and then never finds the love she's looking for? After all, right now she's focused on her own self-development. She wants to finish college and pursue her dream career. Besides, no other guy has made her feel the way he makes her feel.

What's wrong with giving this guy some time to come around?

THINK ABOUT IT...

What do you think she should do?

This young lady must know her guy wants to ice her. And she may be willing to accept it. If a young lady accepts the notion that a guy wants to put her on hold indefinitely, and is willing to sacrifice her enjoyment on the promise that this guy is really going to come back to her when **he's** ready, all I can do is **SMH.**

Here is another situation where a young lady is being iced, but either she doesn't know it or refuses to accept what's happening. She and her boyfriend have been in an off-and-on relationship for quite some time. Through all of their ups-and-downs, they still care deeply for each other. Sometimes their breakups are the result of heated disagreements; it could be because one of them is playfully flirting with someone else (usually him) which upsets the other. Sometimes they don't really know why they break up for a while, they just do.

But each time they have a split, the young man always hooks up with another young woman, while the girlfriend remains loyal. And each time she finds out that he is seeing someone else, they argue again, which extends their breakup. Ultimately, they always find their way back to each other.

The young lady never questions her guy's love for her, and she's all in with him, too. She's so used to the ebb-and-flow of their relationship that she has no doubts about them being together indefinitely. What she is not seriously assessing is the opportunity their separations create for him to fulfill his need for excitement elsewhere. It's not that he doesn't care for her, because he does.

It's just that he doesn't know how to tell her that he really isn't ready for the level of commitment she wants. At the same time, he doesn't want her to move on, and is trying everything he can to keep her on the line, while he does what he wants to do whenever he can.

TALK ABOUT IT...

Do you think she knows she's being iced?

To borrow an old-school expression, a lot of guys want to "have their cake and eat it too!" They want the best of both worlds. A lot of them get away with it because you knowingly allow them to, you're making excuses for their behavior, or you are so clueless that you continue to miss the signs of what is going on.

Icing can be a two-way street! Just like a guy, you can have someone special in your life that you think may have potential in the future, but you are not yet ready for a long-term commitment. You can be open and honest about it with your guy and tell him how you feel. If you two are meant to be together, it will work out; I have seen this happen. In the meantime, lay the groundwork for you to build the best possible life for yourself. When the time is right, the person you have been waiting for will come along.

What guys have to say about putting someone on ice

The practice of putting a young lady on ice may be more common than you want to believe, but you do not have to allow it.

Why do guys do it? They all gave me the same explanation: They don't feel ready for a serious commitment, but if you have the qualities they are looking for in someone to have a serious relationship with, they don't want you to get away. So they say and do just enough to keep you interested and believing that the two of you are really going to be together.

They told me that they know how to be distantly connected, meaning that they text you, call you, and even spend time with you, up to a point. They know how to 'check in' in such a way that they can convince you that you are still #1. Don't let that fool you, because there is a difference between being #1 and being the ONLY one. When guys are using their ice strategies they really have another thing or two going on, if you know what I mean.

The guys I talked with admitted that they want it all—something now plus what they really want for later. So they count on you to stay put while they have the freedom to do what they want elsewhere.

Here's the thing about putting someone on ice ... YOU CAN DO IT, TOO! You can meet a guy and have a strong sense that he may be the man of your dreams. You can like him, love him, and visualize a future with him. On each side, your families may even predict that you will end up together for life. All of that is fine. But at this moment, you may not be ready for a serious commitment. Yet here's the thing:

Unlike a lot of guys, you don't need to play games about it. The reason they do it is because they know they will lose you if they tell you the truth. But when you do it, you are really stepping into your power and taking control of what you are, and are not, ready for. Remember, you really need to spend time focusing on yourself, and laying a foundation for your future. If he's smart, not only will he be working on getting himself together, he will want you to do the same.

Winners, losers, and losses

Have you noticed that guys don't get into fights over girls as much as girls get into fights over guys? Yes, some young men will even get physical over a young woman they care about, but an outright dispute is much more likely among females. Why is that?

Here's an example of an all-too-familiar situation. Two young ladies like the same guy. He's a nice guy, but he's soaking up the attention he's getting from these two. After being entertained by each of them constantly flirting with him, he decides which one he wants to spend time with, which leaves the other one out in the cold. Of course, the one he has chosen is ecstatic! But the other one becomes upset and throws a lot of shade at his new girlfriend on Instagram by suggesting that the only reason he's with her is because "she is nothing more than his slave because she does anything and everything he wants her to."

Of course, all of his new girlfriend's friends begin to *hate* on the one who was kicked to the curb—or did he really kick her off to the side?

A few days later, this guy reaches out to the young lady he *seemed* to have lost interest in. He wants her to know that he can't get her off his mind, and that he really wants to spend time with her "on the low." He adds that "this will be our secret, because we don't need anyone in our business."

But his renewed interest in her is exactly the type of news she needs to get back at his girl, so she posts something in a group text about what happens when a man strays. One of his girlfriend's friends sees the post, reads between the lines, and immediately lets his girl know the latest. Armed with the intel, his girlfriend confronts him, but of course he denies having any knowledge of what she's talking about.

Without hesitation, she believes him, and is now on a mission to deal with her adversary. Once face-to-face, the two young women become embroiled in a nasty, heated, public argument over this guy. Ultimately, he decides to leave both of them alone because he can't deal with the drama. Besides, there's always someone else he can hook up with.

Several months later, these two young women are still posting shady things about each other, even though the guy has walked away.

What guys have to say about NOT trying to win

When I presented this story line to some guys, they laughed and shook their heads because they have seen it play out many times. I asked them to flip the scenario and tell me how this same situation would look if two guys liked the same young lady. This is what they said:

"That wouldn't happen because most guys don't do that. We look at what they (young women) do, and laugh. For us, whoever gets to her first, gets to her first."

This is all they had to say. So, while you are expending your time and energy arguing, doing detective work, and posting your anger on social media, guys keep it simple. No drama, no frills. Give that some thought.

 # Disloyal

There are a few popular songs about young women who cheat on their boyfriends, sometimes with their boyfriend's friend. I never really thought about whether any of these songs are telling true stories until I began talking to some young men who told me story after story about how a young lady they thought had serious girlfriend potential hooked up with one of their "boys," and how devastated they were.

These same guys also said a lot of young ladies engage in this behavior, and that it is more common than many would think. The irony is that some of these young women insist that they are looking for the right guy to have as a boyfriend, while they are being the very thing that the right guy wouldn't want. In fact, these same young ladies would be quick themselves to talk disparagingly about someone who acted this way. But when you're in "It's all about me" mode, I suppose giving thought to the consequences of this behavior (hurting someone, and causing damage to one's own reputation) never enters one's mind. That's kinda' ratchet.

Recently a young man, who was obviously upset that his girlfriend had betrayed him, came to me to talk about her cheating on him with a friend of his. He was so hurt that he called her a THOT. He thought he was doing everything right to show her that he was really into her. She returned his affection with the ultimate disloyalty. He went on to tell me that several young men he knew had the same experience. I found this interesting because I couldn't recall more than a handful of conversations with young women who had admitted to cheating on their boyfriends. I never suspected that this problem was so widespread.

But then I started doing some ear hustling of my own. I overheard several conversations of young ladies who were discussing their own player-like tendencies. Eventually I just asked one of them what was going on with her "bae" and why she felt compelled to cheat. She simply stated that she had "changed her mind." But if she knew that someone was calling her a THOT, she probably would have lost it.

If you are a young woman who is so desperate for attention that you seek it wherever you can find it, **I'm not throwing shade** when I say you can't get upset when your name and THOT are mentioned in the same sentence. I mean no disrespect when I say this to you. I am simply saying this based on the many conversations I have had with young men, and women, who were in-the-loop when someone they knew was seeing someone behind their guy's back. So, don't get mad at me for telling you what others may be saying and thinking about you. Don't get mad at me for telling you that you may ruin your reputation long-term. I'm trying to encourage you to think about the consequences of your decisions.

I also want you to examine why you feel the need to engage in this type of behavior. I can guarantee you that if you are making yourself available to your boyfriend and any friend of his, or if you are being intimate with a guy he doesn't know, whenever he finds out—and it is possible that he will—your image will be tarnished. So, if you are dating a young man but find his friend(s) or other guys attractive to the point that you can't be loyal to the guy you're with, then do him and yourself a favor and leave him alone.

Oh, and there's another thing this young man with the unfaithful girlfriend was upset about. He said that when a guy's girlfriend cheats on him, some people think it's no big deal. They react more when a guy is betraying a girlfriend than they do when it's the other way around.

Breaking the Girl Code

Before moving forward, I need to talk to you about the "Girl Code"—an understanding among women, both younger and more mature, about the rules of female interpersonal relationships. The code makes it clear that certain lines should never be crossed. In other words, there are some things you simply do not do to someone you consider to be a friend. And if you do, your reputation among the young ladies and young men in your social circle can take a hit faster than you can say *thot*!

On multiple occasions, young ladies come to me in distress because someone they considered a friend was obviously flirting with someone they liked. I cannot tell you how many times I have listened to conversations beginning with "She knew I was into him, and as soon as I turned my back she was trying to give him her number," or "She wasn't interested in him until I told her that I liked him," or "As soon as I told her, she started going after him herself."

I have observed young women who seem to have a habit of waiting for one of their friends to attract a guy. When they do, the so-called friends will make their move. They actually try to take the guy away from their friends because they feel it's easier to do that than to be patient for the right guy to come their way. Any of these scenarios is an absolute no-no! Not only is it crossing the line of friendship, it violates another young woman. When you deliberately pursue a guy your friend likes, you are inviting trouble. A young man who finds himself being pursued by a friend of his girlfriend might enjoy the attention. But, more than likely, he will slot her into the Level 1 position.

What guys have to say about ratchetness

Most of the guys I talked to would rather not deal with ratchet behavior. For one thing, it's embarrassing, especially in public. Guys would prefer not to have all eyes on them for the wrong reasons when they are out with you and you're loud, pointing your finger, rolling your neck, and your eyes, all at the same time, and creating a scene because of whatever you may be displeased with.

Another issue with ratchet behavior is that sometimes it puts you and the guy in harm's way. For example, if you get into it with someone over something in this over-the top way I just described, it can lead to your guy having to step in to help settle the matter. And that may lead to someone being harmed physically.

If you take a situation that could have been settled privately or quietly or you could have walked away from, and instead start yelling, screaming, cursing, or whatever, someone on the other side of the argument may choose to retaliate in some over-the-top manner as well. Of course, you believe your guy should now step in and have your back, right? Well, think again. Why should he? Just because he's with you?

Did it occur to you that the problem could possibly have been avoided if you had handled it differently? Oh, I forgot, you're just being you, doing you. Well, yes, it's OK for you to be who you are. But who you are can also realize that sometimes being you causes problems for yourself, and everyone who is associated with you. While there are some guys who get adrenaline rushes from some of the situations you create (I will talk to you about **drama addicts** in a later lesson), most of the guys I have talked to would rather do without it.

The bottom line is that ratchetness isn't attractive and can be a relationship deal-breaker for a lot of young men.

Start out the way you're going to end up

One lesson to learn as early as possible in your dating life is to start off a relationship in the manner in which you want it to evolve, or end up. This means that you have to set the tone of what the expectations will be for yourself and your young man **in the process of getting to know him.** In other words, you should be who you are from the time you meet him. I am not saying that both of you shouldn't try to make a good impression on one another. It's definitely OK to show off your best qualities. It's what most people do when they first meet. What I am saying is that you shouldn't give the impression that you are willing to do any more in the beginning than you are willing to do long-term. You need to start off the way you want to end up.

Let's say that you've just met a young man and both of you have agreed that you would like to get to know each other better. (Remember, this is when the assessment phase begins on your part, and on his.) You immediately try to get on top of your look, which is fine. But then you begin to do too much. You may claim to be interested in the same things he's interested in, when you're not. Subtly, you let him know how much you're willing to be there for him before you know whether he is willing to be there for you. You start getting in over your head trying to prove to him that you're worthy of him before you know whether he is worthy of you. BAD MOVE.

The first time he asks you out, he doesn't have enough to cover the expenses for the evening, so you agree to cover it. The next time he asks you out, he doesn't have any money at all. But you go out with him anyway. You justify paying for it this time because it really isn't that much, and you want him to know that you're in his corner. The next thing you know you have paid for both of you EVERY TIME the two of you go out. And, when you have gotten to the point where you don't want to do it any more, he becomes upset with you because "You have always paid for everything and never complained, so what is the problem now?"

Perhaps you have your own car and either he is saving to get a car, or his car is down right now. So, you agree to do all of the picking up and dropping off, even when it involves some of his friends. Sometimes when he has somewhere to go and you don't have anything to do, he will ask you if you can come over so he can borrow your car for a few hours while you wait at his house with his family. Now, you really feel like you're "in" because, after all, he wants you to spend time with his family while he's not around, which proves that you must be really special to him. After a while this, too, has become a pattern, but it's only after several weeks have passed that you realize he's spending more time with your car than with you. *Hmmmmmm....*

Perhaps you try to show him how smart you are by offering to help with his homework, and before you know it you are doing it for him. But when you tell him that you can't keep doing his homework for him because your grades are dropping, he gets upset because "It was never a problem before." Well, you probably should not have offered to do his homework in the first place.

In a similar situation, I remember a young woman (one of many I have watched sabotage a good relationship) who had just started dating her new boyfriend. He seemed like a nice guy, and they really made a cute couple. But it almost seemed that she had to constantly persuade herself that she was worthy of him. So she kept trying to prove it herself. When he wanted to go out of his way for her, she would tell him that he didn't need to do that because it would be too much for him to take on. When he tried to hold the door open for her, she told him that she could open the door for herself. If she ever seemed upset and he wanted to comfort her, she told him not to worry about her because she would be OK. Are you paying attention to what is happening? Every time he tried to be there for her she wouldn't allow it.

After a few months, the roles in their relationship had reversed. She would go out of her way for him, and he allowed it. He no longer offered to hold the door open for her. Whenever he would have a bad day, she would practically force him to talk to her about what was on his mind, and would become angry when he wouldn't open up to her. Then she began to complain that he didn't seem to care because he never wanted to do anything for her anymore, and she couldn't understand why. Before long, she felt so neglected that she told him she wanted to break up.

THINK ABOUT IT...

What mistake did she make in her relationship?

Some of you may be the type of young lady who feels the need to be in control and to prove you can handle things on your own.

There's nothing wrong with being able to hold your own, but if you are so insistent on being independent you may send the wrong message to the young man you have an interest in spending time with. If you start off your relationship by demonstrating how little you need him to do, please don't complain when he sits back and watches you deal with everything without him. Can you blame him for pulling back?

On the other hand, there are many really cute caring and supportive actions you can take to endear yourself to this guy. You just need to know when to get his back, and when to get your own. Just be honest with yourself about your motives for doing whatever you do. Are you doing these favors to impress him so that you can get him, or are you being your authentic self?

If you're going out of your way and taking special steps just so you can "seal-the-deal," you're setting yourself up for a headache down the line. Obviously, you can't sustain the "I can do it all" behavior. You will crash and take your relationship down in flames with you. Get him started off the way you want to end up by allowing him to show you what he's willing to do to be there for you.

Lesson 7

HE IS WHO HE IS

YOU can't change anyone. A person makes changes in his or her life only when he or she is ready. And it's often difficult. Why am I saying this to you? Because some of you are working hard to change the guy you like to make him who you want him to be.

Even when a guy directly tells you what he does or doesn't want, you are so determined to convince him that you can change him that you are stumblin' and fumblin' and losing control of your own life. You are putting so much of your energy, time, and thoughts into changing him into a "better person" that you are not paying enough attention to you. Remember when I asked you earlier who is into you? If you don't know the answer, whose fault is that? Maybe you're to blame for your own misery. Sometimes your determination puts you in a bad situation.

I'll never forget a conversation I had with two young men who were known "players." Both were dealing with more than one young lady at a time, even while knowing that at least one of the young women really liked them a lot. When I suggested to them they needed to stop playing with the young ladies' emotions before they hurt someone, they explained themselves like this ...

Me: Why do you keep playing with them? You know they're into you.

Guy 1: I keep trying to tell them that I'm not ready to be serious, but they won't listen. So, what am I supposed to do?

Guy 2: (Laughter) I'm into my girl. She's my go-to girl. I'm going to marry her.

Me: Yeah, but is she the only one?

Guy 2: (Lots of laughter!)

Me: Have you told her that you want to marry her?

Guy 2: (Laughter) Yes! (More laughter; this young lady doesn't realize that she's been iced)

Guy 1: You're talking about how you don't want us to hurt them, but we get hurt, too. I've been hurt twice. That's just the way it goes. That's all part of it.

Me: But when you know these girls are into you, you have a responsibility to not lead them on.

Both of them: We try telling them that we aren't ready to be serious, but they don't want to listen. They keep coming at us ... so what are we supposed to do?

OK, ladies, do they have a good question? If you are trying to be the savior of a guy like these to help him change his ways, you really need to listen when he is telling you that he doesn't want to change. He likes the way he is. And why shouldn't he? He is getting exactly what he wants even when he is telling you that he doesn't want it.

In cases like these, truthfully, the guys aren't doing anything wrong; they are simply being who they are. You create problems for yourself when you convince yourself that this guy will change or become a better person because of you. That doesn't work. Remember, a person—including you—only makes changes when he or she is ready. It can't be forced. You may be listening to what I'm saying, but I need you to HEAR ME on this point. Again, you need to **slow your roll.**

There's an old-school expression that goes like this: "If it walks like a duck, and talks like a duck, it's a duck." Some of you are trying to turn ducks into bunny rabbits. It's not gonna happen. I repeat: Stop making your boyfriend a personal project. In some cases, you're doing it so you can feel better about yourself. By this I mean you are pouring yourself into him to "fix him" when you should be trying to enhance yourself. Managing your own life is a full-time job.

Pull yourself together and focus on your own life. Don't sell yourself short; have high standards. You may have to wait longer for the right guy to come along, but if he's right for you he will have been worth the wait.

Get lit, or get bit?

Sometimes you meet a guy and he appears to be really into you, and after a while you stop paying attention to who he really is because he seems to be everything right ... almost too right. He is texting you, calling you, wanting to spend all his time with you. In fact, he seems to be so into you that he doesn't have time for anything else. Week-after-week you two are hangin' tough. In fact, you have lost track of how long this has been going on with this really great guy because this is what you have been waiting on for so long. You look forward to any free time you have to get together with your boo, especially on the weekends so you can *get lit*!!!

In the beginning, it's great! You finally have someone who appears to possess many of the qualities you've been looking for. Your family likes him, and his family seems to like you. He gets along with your friends, and his boys are good with you, too. The two of you are in a world of your own. Even the haters don't stress you out like they usually do. Everything seems to be fine, until ...

One weekend while the two of you are together you tell him that you want to spend next weekend with one of your girls, without him. It could be for any reason; she's going away to college, you want to go shopping or whatever. It really doesn't matter what the occasion is. You just want to hang with your crew because it's something you want to do. All-of-a-sudden, your boyfriend starts to trip! He wants to know why you have to go, especially without him. He may tell you that you didn't mention it to him before you made your plans, and he doesn't like that. He may tell you he doesn't want you to go because he already has something in mind for you two to do together. After all, you always spend weekends with him, so changing things up isn't good.

Now you're really confused because, in your mind, what's the big deal? You're just going to spend time with a friend or two, that's all. You tell him that he needs to "chill and quit trippin'" and that you don't know why he's making a big deal out of nothing.

After the two of you exchange a few heated words, you tell him that you don't care what he thinks because he's not your daddy, and can't tell you what to do. Of course, you add that if he doesn't like it he can ... and then it happens. He grabs your arm and won't let it go. He becomes aggressive, threatens you, and makes clear what will happen to you if you don't do what he says. When you try to pull away, you scream for him to let go of your arm. But your fear and anger only make matters worse. The two of you are making a scene!

So, what happened in this situation? How could such a perfect guy who's so deeply into you turn into this maniac?

Remember, at the beginning I said that, often, when things appear to be going too well, young women don't pay attention to some of the other signs that are present.

When two people are getting to know each other it's natural for each person to be attentive and try to make a good impression. However, there is a big difference between being attentive and being obsessed. Most people in new romantic situations experience a "honeymoon" period. After a few weeks, life seems returns to normal. Whether you're in school, working, or whatever, everyone has responsibilities, friends, hobbies, or something else to do. But in this situation, the young man didn't seem to care about anything except his girlfriend. He wanted to be with her all of the time, then text her, and talk to her as much as possible when they couldn't be together. And the more of her time she gave him, the more he wanted.

If this young lady had been paying attention to some of this guy's habits in the beginning, she might have noticed that some things were out of place. She should have asked herself questions like "Why does he have so much time to text me? Why does he always text me back so quickly? Why doesn't he spend time with his family or friends away from me?" After really giving thought to this situation, another question could be: "Why does he always ask where I am, and what I am doing or who I'm talking to? It's not like he doesn't know because we're together practically all of the time."

In a situation like this, the best decision would have been to not get lit to avoid getting bit! Too often, situations like this can lead to abusive treatment. This abuse can come in many forms. A lot of women in relationships aren't aware that they're being mistreated. If you are being yelled at, called out of your name, physically mistreated, threatened, controlled, or manipulated, you need to get out and possibly seek professional counseling. In extreme cases, you may need legal protection. A lot of mature women who are victims of abuse didn't quickly deal with mistreatment from abusive boyfriends in their younger years. Many women become trapped in a cycle of mistreatment from one guy to the next. If you recognize any signs of abuse, get out right away!

When he tries to control, you need to be BOLD!

A very smart, attractive young lady talked to me extensively about this very issue. She told me she had been dating a very attentive young man for several months. She said they were really into each other, but when she wanted to do something that he didn't want her to do, he grabbed her and pushed her against a wall. She said that she had a hard time getting away from him, and when she did she was shocked and terrified. This is the same guy who had been at her side constantly. If she had known to pay attention to certain signs, she would have **walked away** before things got out of control. Never forget the 30-day rule; I have given it to you for a reason. People always show you who they are. You just have to give them time to do it, and believe what you see when you see it.

Abuse while dating is really a big problem. Quite a few young ladies are involved with young men who are either verbally or physically abusive. Sometimes young ladies tolerate mistreatment because they don't know their self-worth, and sometimes they come from a household where they have either already been abused or have witnessed their mother being abused. As a result, they perceive this treatment as normal instead of the exception. I am telling you now that abusive behavior is never acceptable. At the first sign of any type of abuse, you need to get out. Fast.

For example, if you are getting to know someone and he wants to spend all his time with you, and doesn't seem to care about anything else, this should be a huge warning sign! Most young men who are in high school, college, or beyond have multiple interests. And, as much as they might be into you, many of these guys appreciate having a little time without you. This is totally healthy and natural. In fact, it is healthy for you to have some space of your own so you and he can continue to discover who you are, and how to focus on getting your lives on track. You have the rest of your life to **turn up!** But, for now, pay attention so you will know when to **turn down.**

Recognizing the signs of abuse

Domestic violence is a huge problem in this country, and teen dating violence is no exception. Well over a million teens per year experience violence in their relationships. There are many reasons why this number is alarming; one big factor is that violence has become a part of our culture. There is violence in movies, video games, television shows, and even song lyrics. So it should come as no surprise that violence surfaces in our relationships and in far too many households. Yet, it seems that some of you may not always know some of its characteristics.

Do you recognize abusive behavior when you see it, and do you know what to do about it when it happens? Let's do a quick check to find out. Check off each of the following that you would consider to be some form of potentially abusive behavior.

☐ Being called out of your name under any circumstances.

☐ Having to give details of your whereabouts most of the time.

- [ ] Being isolated from your friends, and sometimes your family, because of what a guy wants.

- [ ] Having to deal with insults and put-downs about your intellect or appearance.

- [ ] Always being made to feel as though you can't do anything right.

- [ ] Openly being insulted in front of his friends or family.

- [ ] Being bruised on more than one occasion while the two of you are just "play wrestling."

- [ ] Not being allowed to have an opinion of your own that differs from his

- [ ] Having to constantly use your resources for the two of you and getting an angry response when you ask him to pay for something.

- [ ] Being encouraged to engage in behavior that goes against your values.

- [ ] Dealing with his anger through physical mistreatment.

- [ ] Constantly being compared to other young women and being told: "I wish you looked more like that."

- [ ] Not being allowed to accept phone calls and text messages when you are with him.

- [ ] A pattern of asking you to prove that you are where you say you are, and that you're doing what you say you are doing.

Well, how many examples on this list did you check? Truthfully, all these could be identified as some form of abusive behavior, even the ones you may think are "cute." You know, those things on this list that allow you to convince yourself that "He really loves me." Let me break it down for you: Love (or really like) does not cause bruises, diminish someone's self-worth, or intimidate. It should never make you feel bad about yourself and/or cause you to question who you are. It doesn't demand that you distance yourself from your friends. It is supposed to empower you and help you become a better person.

I am going to say something now that you may not agree with, but that's never prevented me from offering my opinion before, so why stop now? Sometimes the abuse is coming from your end, and not the young man's. There are a lot of young men who have been subjected to abusive behaviors on the checklist from their girlfriends. They have been insulted, physically attacked, called out of their name, and diminished. These behaviors are inappropriate for young men and they are not justified when a girl is the source of anguish. Abuse is abuse, no matter who is responsible for it.

One young lady told me her boyfriend was mistreating her. Then she asked me if she should tell her mother. Now, this may seem like a no-brainer to you, and you are probably thinking "Of course she should tell." Here's the thing: When a person is being abused a blanket of fear can overtake them, having paralyzing effects. Even the most confident person can become weak under the spell of an abuser, especially if she really cares for the guy. A lot of times women—both young and old—go into the "He doesn't really mean it" or "He's just having a bad day" or "He's going to change" mode. Yeah, right. The lies you tell yourself can be beyond words. So, don't be too hard on that young lady for asking me that question.

So, if I am being abused, what should I do?

Tell someone immediately! At the first sign of mistreatment, you need to end the relationship and GET OUT! Don't give yourself the opportunity for a pattern of mistreatment to set in. Remember, you want to *start off the way you want to end up*. You don't want to send the signal that you are so deep in like or in love that you are willing to tolerate any form of mistreatment. The longer you tolerate it, the worse it may become.

If you are the source of abusive behavior, I suggest that you do a few things: First, you need to ask yourself why you are abusive, and second, you need to get help. If you come from a family where there are obvious abusive patterns, it may be a learned behavioral pattern to which you have been conditioned. Therefore, you don't realize the impact it has had on you. Whether you have been an observer or a victim, getting counseling can help you heal.

Another aspect of abuse that's really frightening is that it can establish a pattern that will follow you into future relationships. I have spoken to countless young women who have been in one abusive relationship after another, on through adulthood.

Here's one example. I know a college student dating a young man who periodically used her as a punching bag. She is smart, attractive, and very capable. Yet she's in a relationship that is totally unhealthy. But when I reflected on her high school boyfriend, I realized that he frequently mistreated her as well. If she isn't careful she will be initiated into the league of women who continually involve themselves with abusive men.

So, remember, if anything I have just said resonates with you, get help, and get out. **DOMESTIC ABUSE HOTLINE: 800-799-7233.**

Self-check: Do you really know what you want in a guy?

What are you looking for in a guy? More importantly, *why* are you looking for these qualities? I'm offering these questions for your consideration because sometimes what we want is based on influences outside ourselves, or deep issues within ourselves. OK. I'm probably confusing you, so let me explain.

Let's look at this from two perspectives, from a guy's and from yours. Sometimes, young men want a young lady for the sake of their ego. They aren't necessarily interested in a real relationship. They just want to have someone who looks a certain way to impress their friends. This situation is obviously being driven by an external influence -- the need to flaunt and show off. But external influences are often driven by internal issues. Why is it so important for some guys to impress their friends? What is it within themselves that causes them to need validation from their crew? Who has made them feel that they're worthless unless they have a particular type of young woman on their arm? Guys can have issues with self-esteem, too.

You, too, may be dealing with influences that determine what you are looking for in a guy, and you are not even aware that they exist. Are you looking for someone just to have someone so you won't be the girl without a boyfriend? Some young ladies just want to be able to say they have a boyfriend because it makes them feel important and special, even if the relationship is dysfunctional. He doesn't text you, you rarely see him, but occasionally he will tell you that he loves you, or whatever. Your need to be able to say that you have someone is all that really matters. If this is the case, you have very limited criteria and expectations. You just want someone to say that you have someone. This is totally an external influence.

But your external influence is being affected by your internal issues. Why do you have to have a guy to make you feel special? Who or what has affected your self-worth? Who has possibly made you feel that you don't have enough going on your own?

Sometimes, if you compare yourself to images in the media—pictures of other women on social media, the internet, magazines, or television, you can easily get the impression that these women have it all! They look fabulous, and you assume they don't have any problems, especially in the dating department. That is so not true! Everyone is dealing with something. Just because these women look like they have it all together doesn't mean they aren't people with stories of their own. They're getting paid or being made popular by what you see. Many of them, just like you, are trying to find their way. It's part of the human condition. Most of us are always trying to figure things out, no matter how old, pretty, rich, famous, or smart we may be.

As you are trying to decide what you're looking for in a guy, you need to determine why you want what you want. At the same time, you have to be the type of person who will be desirable to the type of person you're looking for. You can't afford to be the "nice house, nobody home" type with everything to offer on the surface but nothing going on inside. And, you can't be the desperate type because guys can detect desperation a mile away and will either run from it or possibly manipulate it so they can get what they want before they say "duces" and bounce.

TALK ABOUT IT ...

What do I want in a guy, and why?
In this exercise, really give thought to what you're looking for in a young man. Remember: To like someone who likes you is not enough. Be honest with yourself as you write down the characteristics of your ideal guy.

I want a guy who looks_____,
because_____

I want a guy who likes_____,
because_____

I want a guy who believes in_____,
because_____

I want a guy who is interested in_____,
because_____

I want a guy who values_____,
because_____

So, put forth the effort to *assess* (there's that word again) what is driving your preferences—what you meant when filling in the blanks after "because." Get a handle on your influences. Now, let's look at the other side. Why is it critical to know what you *don't* want in a guy? It's important because when you see signs of those traits you can cut your losses and move on before you become emotionally invested. So let's fill in these blanks:

I don't want a guy who looks_____,
because_____

I don't want a guy who likes_____,
because_____

I don't want a guy who believes in_____,
because_____

I don't want a guy who is interested in_____,
because_____

I don't want a guy who values_____,
because_____

You are entitled to wanting what you want, and not wanting what you don't want. At the end of the day, it is your relationship. However, you have to accept the consequences of whatever you choose to deal with.

Lesson 8

HE'S NOT YOUR DADDY, AND YOU ARE NOT HIS MAMA!

Unfortunately, you may have been raised without your father in your life. This is the sad reality for many young women (and young men). The absence of a father figure leaves a gaping hole in your life. You may have lost your dad because of a tragedy, such as death, or another reason that has caused a disruption. Perhaps your dad just didn't want the responsibility of being a parent. For whatever reasons, he is simply no longer a part of your life.

Another possibility is that you may be in a situation where your mom has married someone and you now have a stepfather who is supposed to be the daddy in your life. Perhaps you do not accept him in this role, even if he is trying to be the best dad possible. After all, it's not easy being a replacement for the real thing. On the other hand, he might be more concerned with his relationship with your mom, and preoccupied with his own biological children, if he has any. Or maybe he is not being a responsible parent toward them either. The bottom line is that with any of these scenarios you feel empty because you are being deprived of being "daddy's little girl."

No matter how much you may long for your dad—or for someone willing to be your dad—whatever guy you choose to like will not be a replacement for your father, so don't expect him to fill that void. It is not his responsibility to play multiple roles in your life. You cannot demand that he make you the focal point of his world, spend all his time thinking about you, and spoil you beyond measure. If you have unrealistic expectations of him, and he can't fulfill them, you'll resent him and any guy who follows him. Eventually, you could develop an attitude of resentment toward men. As you enter adulthood, this negative outlook will create problems for you in your future relationships.

And, just as you cannot expect him to fill the daddy void, don't try to be his mother. Whether he knows his real mom or not, he doesn't need you to be one for him. You don't always need to remind him to do his homework or do it for him. You don't always need to run errands for him, or spoil him with expensive gifts to show your affection. You don't always need to help him to be more organized. He will need for you to be in his corner, but not be his keeper.

What you want is a young man who knows how to be a man. The problem is that many of them don't really know how to be one because they are missing their fathers, too. No one has shown them what being a man looks like. And some of them resent their own mothers—if they are around—and have a quiet resentment toward women. Any guy who does not respect his mother is incapable of respecting you. This is why you need to **slow your roll and wait 30 days** to discover who he is, and where he's coming from. This waiting period will also give you time to get your head together to know what your role should and shouldn't be if the two of you get together.

I'm not saying you shouldn't be a "good girlfriend." What I'm saying is that you should be clear in your mind that he can't fill that open daddy's space in your heart, and that being his mother is simply not your job. Be supportive, yes. Be unrealistic and excessively nurturing, no.

What guys have to say about being mothered, and playing daddy

Guys really need to be allowed to find their way. Many of them have told me that they don't mind you getting their back, but they really need to do what they want to do; they need to pursue their dreams and their interests. A lot of times, their dreams and interests may not include you. And sometimes they just need their space. If they feel too crowded too frequently, they will begin to pull away.

"I need some space"

Let's define the word "space." In the context of a relationship, space for a guy means something totally different from what it means to you. To a guy, space means having the freedom to do what he wants, when he wants. It means not having to discuss everything and every thought or decision with you. It doesn't mean that he doesn't like you. It means having room to breathe, without any consequences. When you know how to properly create this space it enhances your *mystique,* which we will talk about in greater detail in a later lesson.

Now, for you the word "space," when you hear it from him, probably means something entirely different. For you, it means that he wants to end the relationship, or that he wants to take a break. Perhaps to you it means he has met someone else and doesn't know how to tell you that he wants to move on. Sometimes your assessment is correct, but sometimes it's not. If you tend to be needy and don't have many interests beyond him, you have made him the center of your existence. You may be crowding him without even realizing it. On the other hand, if you are too distant, he may think you are not that interested, and after trying unsuccessfully to work things out with you he might just "ease on down the road."

The bottom line is that the word will have a different meaning depending on how you interpret it. Before you start freaking out when you hear "space," perhaps you should have a calm conversation to try to understand what the deal is.

Two-way communication is not a one-way street

Clear communication is the cornerstone of any good relationship. And just like with driving, you have to share the two-way road. In this case, the road is your relationship. You have to learn how to anticipate what may cause a roadblock. Sometimes you have to yield to the other person. In other words, it's not all about you, boo.

Sometimes young ladies are so wrapped up in their own world that they don't fully engage and acknowledge the other person. You misread the traffic signs and make assumptions while talking to your guy about where his head is. Rather than listening, some of you hurl accusations, give ultimatums (it's never a good idea to do this), and ask your guy questions but don't allow him to answer. And when he does answer, you tell him what he's saying isn't true and you accuse him of lying. (Sometimes he may be doing just that, but we'll cover this later.)

The bottom line is that you have to develop effective communication skills. Being able to listen is an extremely important part of this skill. After you have explained how you feel and what's on your mind, you have to be prepared to pause, and **listen**. You have to listen to hear what is being said, and **what is not being said**. When you ask questions, don't be upset when he gives you an answer that you may not want to hear. If you want honest responses to your questions, you should be honest, too. No yelling and screaming. No emotional meltdowns. Just listen, and learn.

And pay attention to the body language of your guy because it will speak volumes about how connected he is to your discussion. Hopefully, he will be all-in. If he's not, don't take that personally, either. You can't force someone to communicate if he isn't ready to do it. If this happens, take responsibility for your part in this process. Remember, you can take advantage of having some "space" yourself.

Finally, in the process of communicating you should put forth an effort to be *transparent*. What do I mean by this? I mean that you should be clear about your intentions when you communicate so you are not sending mixed signals. Mean what you say, but say what you mean. Guys hate playing guessing games with you.

What guys have to say about guessing games

Guys hate to guess why, when, and where something has gone wrong. They can tell when something is bothering you. When they ask and you say "I don't want to talk about it," they watch you walk around with an attitude, forcing them to try to guess what the problem is. And then if they don't continue to ask what's wrong, you accuse them of not being concerned. They don't know whether they've done something wrong or if something else is going on. They need you to talk to them, or resolve the issue so they don't have to deal with your moodiness. Too many of these ups and downs without explanation can drive a guy away.

The other thing is that when you sense something is wrong with them, you ask them over and over again to talk to you, which is something you won't do for them. Then, you assume you are the reason they are upset, and you begin talking to your "girls" about the problem when you don't know what is going on yourself. All of this creates unnecessary confusion. Don't expect guys to talk to you about what's on their mind simply because you want them to put your mind at ease that you are not the problem. Stop pressing them to talk to you on demand. Just be encouraging. Being positive can go a long way.

Remember, effective communication is the foundation of *any* good relationship. Be mindful of your intentions and stop the guessing games in order to get attention.

Lesson 9

THE RELATIONSHIP SCALE: YOU'RE AT A 5, BUT HE'S AT A 1

So, you begin talking to this guy, and he's doing all the right things. He is being attentive, he is being affectionate, and he wants to spend time with you rather than with his friends. For your part, you've been in girlfriend mode for quite a while; you were just waiting for him to catch up! You two are officially a couple.

OK, a few months go by and you continue to do all the things you were doing in the beginning, and possibly more. On the relationship scale, you're likely at a five, maybe a four. But I can almost assure you that if you have been seeing this guy for a few months and his behavior toward you is changing, on the scale he is probably more like a one or two.

What happened? Why did things change? The truth of the matter is that most teenage guys simply don't have the capacity to be super-serious with a young lady for a prolonged period. Of course there are positive exceptions, but most of the young men I have talked to tell me they just cannot be as serious as you are. They may like you—and they don't want to hurt your feelings—but they're tired of living up to your "boyfriend expectations." This means they want out. Now, if you still offer him certain benefits (you probably know what I mean, and I do not advocate this) he will hang around you, but for the wrong reasons. If you allow yourself to be a convenience just to hold on to him that's not a smart move. To be honest with you, when you see a change in his behavior toward you, that's a likely indication that he has already moved on.

Some guys simply don't like the responsibility of doing "boyfriend work." Being a boyfriend might sound like a good idea at first, but once they get into it and realize your expectations, they're ready to call it off. Here's the thing: You are thinking long term, and they don't think that far down the road at this age. If you are both in your teens, maybe a serious commitment shouldn't be on your mind, or his, at this point.

Young ladies have such romantic notions about relationships. You meet a guy, you are attracted to him, and then you think about possibilities for the future. And, while you are daydreaming about that, they are looking for the hottest gym shoe or video game to drop.

I had a conversation with two young men who were high school seniors preparing for graduation. At the time, both had girlfriends who were placing demands on them and creating too much pressure. The young ladies who were dating these two guys constantly wanted their attention. They corrected the guys whenever they thought the guys were doing something wrong—like they were their mothers, not their girlfriends. They wanted the guys to conform to their expectations, and were prone to creating loud, sometimes public arguments (you know, that Reality TV behavior) when they didn't get their way. The guys really liked their girlfriends, but wanted out of their relationships. They were trying to hold on through prom night, which they knew would guarantee a "good time" before they "bounced."

What guys have to say about bossy young women

Several of the young men I've talked to wonder why young ladies feel as though they have the authority to tell them what to do. In fact, one young man said, "I don't know why she thinks that I am supposed to be her personal assistant." Apparently, a lot of guys feel that a bossy, demanding attitude seems to emerge when some of you are in a relationship with them. They resent the fact that you become controlling and insist on only having your way. Perhaps your intention is not to cause any problems, but acting this way is turning a lot of guys off. It makes you appear self-centered and self-absorbed. If you tend to be this way, you may want to consider making some adjustments.

The flip side of all of this is that some of you are so concerned about the young men in your life you feel compelled to be super-supportive. This is fine with them, up to a point. Some of them feel that in your effort to inspire them you sometimes go overboard and start telling them what they must do. Now, for example, if you tell them they aren't moving along with their lives as fast as you think they should be, they understand that you mean well, but sometimes this can be too much.

So this is a time when good communication between the two of you is very important. Rather than offering your unsolicited, constructive criticism, perhaps you should ask your guy how you can be supportive. If you ask, and he tells you, then you can decide if his suggestion is reasonable for you. You don't have to comply with his request if it won't work for you. Remember, as we discussed in the lesson about communication, you want to be transparent. You don't want to agree to doing something that you will later resent. It is important for you to get his back without riding on his back. So keep the communication going toward what's best for both of you.

Guys won't always tell you, but they have self-esteem issues, too

Believe it or not, there are a lot of young men who don't feel that good about themselves. Like many of you, they question whether they are good enough and smart enough. They can feel uncertain about their looks, their style, and their ability to attract the right young lady into their lives. I have watched young men gaze and stare at young ladies across a room with a look of total hopelessness. Some of these guys are still "under construction," meaning they still have a lot of work to do to get themselves together for themselves, not to mention being together enough to approach you. Some of them really deserve a shot but because they doubt themselves—and have observed how you have treated and have talked about people in general —they decide that they are not together enough to "step to you."

Here's the thing: Some of these guys have the very qualities and type of character you say you want! But they have watched you and have *ear-hustled* while you have been talking to your friends enough times to know what you're looking for in a guy. So they just give up because they don't think they will ever measure up.

I'm not suggesting that you should give serious consideration to every guy who's interested in you. I'm just explaining that guys can have the same insecurities that a lot of young women have. And, sometimes, because you can so easily focus on the type of young man who may not be the best for you, you overlook someone who may be a better fit. Remember, you need to assess! You want to be sure that you're not missing out on a great friendship, or more.

What guys have to say about their self-esteem

The young men I have talked to about self-esteem issues all agreed that having or not having a father in their life has a profound impact on the way they feel about themselves. Often, they resent the fact that they haven't been given the guidance they need to develop into the type of young men they want to become. Although most of the guys I have talked to seem to have a healthy respect for their grandmothers, mothers and sisters, they yearn for a male role model they can admire and emulate. As with many of you, the void in their lives is profound. But, because society is not tolerant of young men who cry and are emotional, they bury their feelings and try to act as if they aren't hurting, when they are.

This doesn't mean they need a young woman to mother them. Just as a guy can't replace a father who is missing from a young woman's life, you can't love and mother a young man into feeling better about himself because his father is missing. Young men just want you to know how their self-esteem is affected by this in ways you will never understand. So, keep this in mind when you are dating someone you really care about.

Another point that young men want to make is that they have difficulty feeling good about themselves when you're constantly criticizing them because of what they don't have. Not all young men have a great sense of fashion, reliable transportation, or whatever it is **you** think they should have. They sometimes feel that your main interest is to change them into what you want them to be, which never seems to be enough.

A young man's feelings of self-doubt may be no different than yours, whether he admits it or not. If you can't treat him with respect, do him a favor and just leave him alone.

Lesson 10

READING THE SIGNS OF "I'M OUT!"

When a guy has decided that he wants to move his life in a direction away from you, he may not know how to tell you that. To make matters worse, you don't always read the signs. In many instances when a young man seems to be disconnected, you immediately assume you have done something wrong to cause him to become distant. You go into the "I'm going to fix it" mode, which makes it even harder for him to tell you he simply wants to take a break. Sometimes his shift in feelings is due to the pressures of a committed arrangement. Sometimes it's due to a wandering eye (he has met someone else who has piqued his interest). And sometimes it can be because it's too difficult to figure you out. The bottom line is that something has caused him to change his mind about being in a relationship with you. He wants out.

Here's the thing: He may really care about you although he doesn't appear to be interested anymore. He cares about you enough to try to avoid hurt feelings as he walks away. The problem is that you refuse to recognize all the clear signals that he's no longer interested in being part of your world.

Here's what you need to know about how to recognize that a guy may be "out":

- He abruptly stops texting and face-timing you.
- He stops responding to your text messages.

- He constantly sends your calls directly to voicemail.
- You have to track him down to find out why you haven't heard from him and he tells you that he's been "busy," with no other explanation.
- He doesn't have time to spend with you because he's working or studying hard for a test ALL THE TIME.
- He suddenly says he has to assume responsibility for his family, all day, seven days a week.
- You hear that he is trying to hook up with someone else, or already has.
- He tells you he wants to see you but never follows through.
- Whenever you go by his house to talk to him, he's not there. And you leave a message but he doesn't get back to you.
- He reaches out to you only when he needs something; not only is he "out," you're being used.
- If you think you should make yourself available just to show him how much he needs you, you are asking to be used and you're not accepting the reality that he really is out.

If a guy has decided he's no longer interested, FOR WHATEVER REASON, let him move on! Sometimes guys are in experimental mode to find out what they like, and don't like. Sometimes they simply want to try a different flavor. And, sometimes, you are so intense about the relationship that they feel smothered and need to escape so they can breathe. Whether or not there is something you have or have not done before, is not the issue. If he has decided that he doesn't want to be with you anymore, let him go.

This is krazy!!!
One young man told me he was contemplating ways to fake his death so he could get a young lady to leave him alone. TRUE STORY! He said he had explained to her repeatedly that he wasn't interested in her, but she said he was in denial and insisted that they were destined to be together. When I suggested that he simply

block her phone number, he said "She knows where I live. Blocking her number won't solve the problem."

Now, I'm sure you are thinking that either he is so into himself he has a seriously distorted understanding of what is really going on, or the young lady who seems to be stalking him has a serious problem. If you choose the latter of these two options, you're probably right. But here's the thing. There are a lot of young women who so desperately want to be involved with a specific guy they become totally irrational. I have seen this occur in varying degrees when a young lady does not read the signs of He's Out. To be honest with you, sometimes a guy is never In to begin with. When you don't "assess so you won't be a mess" and don't apply the 30-day rule or something similar to slow you down until you are sure that both you and the guy you like are on the same page, you can be swept away and enter a U-ship without knowing it.

I know of several other situations where young men have kept explaining that they were either "out" or not interested from the beginning, but the young women would simply not take that for an answer. In each of these cases the young women were over-the-top with their pushy insistence that they were going to make the target of their affections change his mind.

One young man told me about a young woman he had ended a relationship with who physically attacked him because she "loved" him. I don't know about you, but anyone who loved me that much would have to explain their feelings to the authorities after I had filed for a restraining order. It's true that love can drive you to do things you wouldn't ordinarily do. But if you know someone who believes in *extreme love* or *loving hard,* encourage them to talk to someone who can help them process their emotions in a healthier way.

THINK ABOUT IT...

What makes young women lose so much control of their emotions and what drives them to behave in such a violent manner?

Don't be judgmental and critical as you process this question. Think about this from your heart, not from your head.

Rejection vs. not being a good fit

Sometimes when a guy no longer seems interested, consider the possibility that you are no longer a good fit for him. You allow yourself to feel rejected when it may not really be that deep. Perhaps he isn't a good fit for you anymore, either. But you want to be in a relationship, and so you will push to make it work even though you know in your heart that the situation is no longer for you.

It's kind of like a pair of shoes that you really wanted but when you tried them on they weren't as comfortable as you had hoped. But you bought them anyway and proceeded to tell yourself they felt great. In reality, they were never a good fit. You wore them simply because you liked the way they looked and you wanted them so badly. OMG they were uncomfortable! But you kept on wearing them until you really couldn't take it anymore, so either you put them in the back of your closet or you give them away. It's nothing personal against the shoes; they simply did not work for you. So get your head together and move on. You have more to look forward to than you know.

The self-blame game

Every time something appears to be out of sync between you two it does not mean you have done something wrong. OMG. I cannot count the number of young women over the years who spiraled out of control with feelings of "What did I do wrong? Was it something I said?" whenever things weren't going smoothly.

STOP IT! It may have nothing to do with you. Maybe he has a few private concerns or troubles. If he does, he has the right to keep his thoughts to himself until he's ready to share them, if ever. (Don't badger him by asking "What's wrong?" over and over again. I know you're concerned, but it may not give you the results you're seeking.)

Perhaps the relationship has run its course. Maybe (just like the shoes) it was never a good fit to begin with. Who knows? The bottom line is that you shouldn't automatically assume you're the cause of problem. When women of any age do this, we begin to have internal dialogues that cause us to question ourselves. If you begin doing this at a young age, it may become a habit that you'll find hard to break later in life. It's fine to examine what's happening or may have happened between the two of you. But the key words here are the **two of you**. A meaningful relationship involves two people. Each person must own his or her part in the ups and downs.

As you reflect on your contributions and other steps that have led you to where you are, you have the ability to self-correct and make adjustments as you move forward. If moving forward doesn't include him, learn from your experience and let go. You will have many more encounters on your journey to find *the right one*.

Lesson 11

THE BOOMERANG EFFECT: WHEN GUYS TRY TO COME BACK

So, you have been in a relationship for however long, and you have seemingly done everything right. You have been your authentic self, not putting up a front to be someone you're not. You've been kind, supportive, and attentive, and not too pushy. You maintained your friendships with your "girls" and spent time with them while you encouraged your guy to hang out with his "boys." Your family really likes him, and his family really likes you. Then, all of a sudden, BOOM! The relationship hits a wall and comes to a screeching halt.

You try to talk to him about what's going on, but he really doesn't have any logical explanation to give you (perhaps you missed some of the signs that he's out). You're upset, broken-hearted, and you feel that you're being treated unfairly. You call your "girls" for advice and they give the situation mixed reviews: Some say he probably just needs some space while others call him a list of unkind names and affirm that you're too good for him and that he doesn't deserve you. (Oh, be careful who you call your friends because I have seen situations where the very friend who claims to have your back is simply waiting for her chance to make her move. When you and your bae are no longer together she's the first person blowing up his phone with text messages to let him know that she's there for him, too, if you know what I mean.)

So, after time has passed you're getting over him. You are finally at a point when you don't think about him all the time, and it feels great! You have moved on to the next great thing in your life, and out of nowhere he sends you a text message just to say "hey." When he does this, part of you is surprised, yet happy to hear from him, part of you is reminded of how he hurt you, and another part is upset that he would even dare to text. But, because you're curious, you go ahead and respond to his message to find out what he wants. He replies: "You were just on my mind." After a few texts fly back and forth, you decide that you are too busy to deal with him right now—whether you're really busy or not—and end the conversation.

Here's the thing ... he starts texting you again in the next day or two. The text messages start off the same way and seem casual, but then he says he wants to see you. When you ask him why, he says something like "I've been thinking" and wants you to give "us" another chance. When he does this you need to duck, because the boomerang is coming your way.

The boomerang effect happens when a couple breaks up, only for one of them to discover that what they had was better than anything they have encountered since then. It's a realization that, in hindsight, while your relationship may not have been perfect, it had the potential to develop into something meaningful. So a guy realizes he has messed up by letting a good thing get away.

The guys' comeback may be slow, but a lot of times they will make a strong attempt to get back in the saddle. Sometimes this is where the 80/20 relationship rule applies, which is the theory that in a good relationship you're only going to get 80% of what you want. The challenge for some guys is that they sacrifice the 80% and wind up with only 20% with the next person. This is when they attempt to boomerang back to you. But you are in control! You can use power moves that will help you keep yourself, not him, in check.

What are power moves?

A power move is a move that keeps you in control of yourself. The objective is not to control the other person, because that can become a huge distraction, or a full-time job! What you should want to do is manage your own thoughts, actions, and responses. If you properly manage your thoughts it will help you control your actions and your responses to situations as they arise.

Let me explain the process of moving toward using power moves. Once you have stopped mourning the loss of your relationship and are regrouping, you should reflect on the highs and lows of the time you invested with your former guy. You should assess what worked well, and what could have worked better. If you are honest with yourself, you may be able to admit how you may have played a role in contributing to the demise of your relationship.

Now, you may be thinking that you didn't do anything wrong while the two of you were together, and that it was entirely his fault that things fell apart. Well, I disagree with this way of thinking. It takes two people to make a relationship work, and two to contribute to it not working. Sometimes a contribution may be as simple as having chosen to become involved with the wrong person for you in the first place. Remember my example of the pair of shoes that hurt your feet? If you don't assess and keep your eyes wide open, you may walk into a relationship that was doomed from the beginning.

But let's talk about your guy who has decided to attempt to boomerang back into your life after you have finally managed to stop thinking about him all the time. When you decide to respond to his request to see you, as many of you will, you need to have your head on so that you don't become weak for whatever he may be saying, or attack him because he broke your heart. Here is a list of potential power moves you can make:

1. Be pleasant. Why should you be otherwise? He probably already knows that the breakup hit you hard. Besides, you have agreed to see him, so you should give him a big hug and a smile! What do you gain from sitting with a bitter attitude? What purpose will it serve? You have been assessing your former relationship all this time, so you know not only what he may have done, but you have been honest with yourself and have admitted whatever you may have done. Being honest with yourself takes courage, but it is also empowering! It will keep you from being defensive when you sit and talk to him. Not only that, he may be expecting you to be bottled-up, on edge or negative. Being pleasant keeps you in control, while throwing him off guard.

2. Listen. Staying calm and cool while listening to what he has to say is empowering. He may attempt to be sincere or he may offer the same tired explanations that sounded reasonable while you were together. You wanted to believe him, but now that you have taken time to assess, you listen with new ears. Even if you still care about him, you approach the conversation from a different perspective. Active listening will help you hear exactly where he's coming from. Then you can decide whether you want to give him a second chance.

3. Pull up, step back. Don't get emotional. When you do, you won't be able to listen or thoughtfully respond. Don't let your thoughts trigger you to lose control. Tell him how you feel, just do not lose control in the process. Have an out-of-body experience. Step back and look at the situation as though you are not sitting in the middle of it, so that you can detect the subtle nuances that may be going on. While he talks, is he looking at you or looking away? Is he checking his phone or is he trying to connect with you? If you pull up and step back, you may observe things about him that are more of a turn-off than a turn-on. That's when you can let go and laugh inside because you see that it's not that deep, and neither is he!

4. The decision is yours! Whether you decide to give your ex another chance is entirely up to you. Your thorough assessment should help you conclude whether you want to travel down the road with him again. If you decide that it's best for you to move on, that's awesome! And, if you decide to go back for round 2, that's awesome too, as long as you go in with your assessment tools, and with your eyes wide open. Keep in mind that no matter what he says, he probably hasn't changed that much since you two broke up, but if you have been working on how to make thorough assessments, you have changed!

Lesson 12

SO, HOW IS THAT WORKING FOR YOU? TAKING ADVICE FROM THE WRONG PEOPLE

When you have a problem that you want to discuss, where do you go? Do you go to your social media and blast your business? Do you talk to your girls? Whose advice are you taking when it comes to your relationship, and other personal issues?

I hope you really hear me on this point. You absolutely need to be mindful of what you share, and who you share it with. Some of the people in your inner circle may be fine. But when it comes to your boyfriend, there are some young ladies who are so ratched that they will give you advice while they are plotting to take advantage of whatever you may tell them and will ultimately stab you in the back. The next thing you know, they are with your ex-boyfriend.

You can't tell everyone everything. And, you can't trust everybody. You really have to assess so you won't be a mess in this case. If you are not careful you will wind up in a ball of confusion that you created yourself because you shared too much with too many people, or the wrong people. By the way, publicizing your personal matters in group texts, Instagram or Twitter can cause extensive damage to your reputation that may take you years into your adulthood to repair.

Wherever you put your ear determines what you may hear!

You can benefit from having a few *besties*—trusted friends—who can be your sounding board. Notice I used the words **trusted**

friends. How do you define friendship? What are your criteria for calling someone a friend? Real friendships do not form overnight. The only way to know if you can trust someone is experience. Over a period of time, they demonstrate that they are worthy of your trust.

You also need to check out the lives of the people you're seeking out for advice. If they can't get themselves together, what makes you think they can advise you on anything? Sure, they can listen to you. Anyone can do that. But the ability to give sound advice is an entirely different matter. Sometimes other young women are so miserable themselves that they will give you advice based on their own bitterness. And there are some young women who talk about **themselves and their problems** so much that you never get a chance to share what's on **your** mind. Wherever you put your ear determines what you will hear!

The other thing is that you have to be a friend to have a friend. So, don't be the young lady who doesn't know how to listen to someone. Don't be the young lady whose life is always a mess. Don't be the young lady who is so bitter that everything you have to offer is mean and hateful. Is this you? If so, it's time to assess. And if you don't fit this description, that doesn't mean it doesn't apply to any of your "girls."

If you have a friend who has difficulty getting along with people and has never had a successful relationship, it's probably not a good idea to turn to her for advice. I'm not saying that it's impossible for her to offer food for thought, but always consider the source of your information. You don't want to be like a woman who has children taking advice about how to raise kids from someone who doesn't have any. Or like taking scuba diving lessons from someone who can't swim.

Once you are comfortable that you have the right support system to get you through the rough patches, please remember what I said earlier about relationships being a two-way street. This comment applies to all of your relationships. In other words, if you want people to listen to you, you have to be able to listen as well.

Friends will ask your opinion and, if you trust them enough, you'll ask for their opinion. You and your girls might find it helpful, at this point, to try out some new texting options. Here are a few that can help make your messages strong and clear.

DH: Dump Him! Have you ever known someone who is dealing with a guy she never should have become involved with in the first place but keeps trying to make it work? Perhaps you have a friend whose boyfriend has done something totally unspeakable and she just needs to let him go. Or, you keep giving a friend the same good advice, but she says she "loves him" and refuses to get a clue? In scenarios like these, a simple **DH** may be appropriate.

YDB: **You Deserve Better.** A friend of yours keeps tolerating her boyfriend's fickle ways; one day he is into her, the next day he doesn't seem to care. You watch your friend ride on the rollercoaster with this guy a few times, but she can't see that the longer she stays on the ride the more likely it is that she's going to get hurt. So, send her a **YDB** to help her wake up. You hope the YDB will shock her into disconnecting from this guy and opening up to the possibility of someone new.

WWYT: Why Waste Your Time? Perhaps you have met a young man, and after a few text messages, and some FaceTime, you have decided that he might be the kind of guy you have been hoping to meet. But the more you hang around him, the more you realize he's really not your type. However, he's nice and has **potential** (be careful if you feel this way, because sometimes the young man can become more of a project than a boyfriend). Yet, your lives are on two different trajectories. You are focused on your goals, but he doesn't have any.

A friend of yours sees this and sends you the text **WWYT**? to bring you back to reality! Why would you spend time hoping for things to go well between you and this guy when you already know you are on separate tracks? You have more important matters to be concerned about. Don't waste your time with a going-nowhere relationship.

JLHA: Just Leave Him Alone. Your boyfriend seems to have lost interest in being with you. He rarely texts you, has stopped FaceTiming you, and takes a long time to respond to you when you reach out to him. Yet you keep blowing up his phone with text messages, and stalk him on social media. You begin to post desperate messages on Instagram telling him off, and making your private matters concerning him public. You're becoming a mess, because you refuse to assess.

One of your friends who knows you well sends you a **JLHA.** This would be good advice. If a guy has become distant, blowing him up and talking about him in chatrooms is not going to make matters better. In fact, it will likely drive him farther away because now he is dealing with a psycho (yes, that would be you) who won't leave him alone. And, everyone on social media who is witnessing your meltdown will know you have lost it. When your text message says **JLHA**, that will probably be the best thing to do.

SHTV: Send Him to Voicemail! In an earlier lesson, I encouraged you to read the signs of "he's out," which included paying attention to how frequently your guy sends you directly to voicemail. Well, you have the same option when you have decided you're out!

Let's say your boyfriend has become distant. You have exhausted all methods of keeping everything together between the two of you, but things still aren't working. As the distance between the two of you continues to grow, you gradually accept that's its over, and you begin the process of healing your heart and letting go. When you are almost able to breathe a sigh of relief that you are over him, he calls you! Because you have a weakness for him, you answer. He explains that he has been thinking about you, and wants to know when the two of you can talk.

You immediately call one of your girls, and she reminds you that unless he has REALLY changed in the last few days, he's the same person who had been totally ignoring you. She goes on to advise you that he just likes the idea of keeping you hanging, simply because he can. Then she directs you to be strong, and **SHTV**. If he's truly serious, he won't give up trying to connect with you. If he gives up after a few attempts, he isn't genuinely interested.

On the other hand...

You may be the type of handle-her-own-business young woman who can put a guy in check and keep him there once your relationship is over. So, here are a few texting expressions for you:

NMP: Not My Problem

YWBOK: You Will Be OK

An old-school expression says "You never miss your water 'till the well runs dry." In other words, you don't miss what you had until it's gone. Sometimes a guy realizes that he has really messed up after the two of you have broken up, and he is trying to get you back by texting you sad stories that will make you feel sorry for him in an effort to get your attention (the Boomerang Effect we saw in Lesson 11). He reaches out to you about whatever challenge he's having, not that he is asking you to do anything about it, but he just wants you to know.

In this case, you have the option of either not responding at all—which sends a powerful message itself—or you can hit him with **NMP**, because unless you are interested in being hooked back in, whatever is going on with him really isn't your problem. And then you add **YWBOK**, meaning that whatever is going on, he will find a way to manage it. These two expressions are empowering when you can send them, and mean it.

And last, but not least, there is always the option to respond with **IDC: I Don't Care!**

Lesson 13

WHO'S INTO YOU?

My aunt taught me, years ago, that when it comes to dealing with guys, if you're into him and he's into himself, who is into you? I was recently talking to a young lady about the challenges she was having with her boyfriend. She said she really loves him, but he never calls, he never comes over, they never go anywhere together, he lacks ambition, he doesn't care about school, and every time they break up he spends time with other young ladies. Despite all this, his parents absolutely adore her because she is positive, progressive and a good student who has definite goals.

While she was telling me this, I was thinking to myself, *and you love him because...?* Eventually I had to stop her and make her listen to what she was telling me. I had her write down everything she had said, and made her read it out loud. After she read it, she realized there was nothing positive on her list.

I suggested to her that, perhaps, she loved this guy because he had become a habit. It was easier to like him and tolerate his indifference than let him go and wait for someone better to come along. Of course, she responded that she didn't want to be alone. The truth is, she was ALREADY ALONE! Her young man was not around most of the time and the picture she had painted of her relationship was all in her mind.

Let's define relationship. A relationship is the way in which two or more concepts, objects, or people are connected, or the state of being connected. Based on this definition, she is not in a relationship because there is no connection.

Giving it up: the habit of self-sacrificing

Many of you have the tendency to make sacrifices to keep your boyfriend happy. For example, perhaps you two have planned to go to dinner and the movies. You have been looking forward all week to seeing this movie with him. You have chosen the perfect outfit and told all your friends about your great weekend plans. But at the last minute he sends you a text telling you that **he** would rather go bowling and that he wants the two of you to do that instead. OK … no problem. You really want to spend time with him, so you're willing to be flexible. You go bowling together, and you have a really great time.

The following week it happens all over again. You agree that on the weekend the two of you will go to a friend's family picnic. Once again, you take your time selecting the perfect outfit, and you tell your friend whose family is hosting the picnic that you and your guy will definitely be coming. On the day of the picnic he picks you up and announces that he would much rather go to his friend's softball game, and wonders if you would be willing to do that instead. You take a deep breath, and, once again agree to go along with the new plan, even though it's not what you want to do and committed to do. But you justify going with him to the game because "at least he is spending time with me." Then more changes in plans happen, and before you know it you have no voice, no input and no decision-making power in the relationship. Instead, you're "giving it up."

Giving it up and making sacrifices for the sake of the relationship should be mutual. It's OK sometimes to agree to a change in plans. However, your young man has to be equally willing to make adjustments as well. If you are always trying to accommodate him and he doesn't demonstrate a willingness to do the same thing for you, you just might be giving away all of your power.

Unfortunately, this is something that affects far too many young women.

If you are constantly giving up and giving in to keep the relationship alive, you may need to reassess your situation.

Let's look at another scenario. Perhaps you have to study for tomorrow's test and you need to spend most of your evening reviewing your notes. Your boyfriend knows you have to study because you have been talking about it all week. In fact, he has the same instructor and should be preparing as well. As soon as you get into your study zone, he sends you a text message telling you that he misses you and wants to talk. You respond by telling him that you really need to stay focused. You explain that you'll be applying for college soon, and you have to do your best in all of your classes. But he sends you another text message telling you that he misses you, and if you really cared about him you would spare a few minutes.

THINK ABOUT IT ...

What would you do?

As much as you may really want to talk to him, can you afford the time away from your studies? Remember, he **knows** you have to study for a test! Why would he try to distract you? And why would you let him?

You already know what happens next. You melt when he tells you that he misses you, and that if you really cared about him you would call him, so he can hear your voice. If you have the discipline to talk for just a few minutes and then get back to your books, that's fine. The problem is that once you begin talking to him you lose track of time. The two of you are laughing and talking, and checking out videos on YouTube together. The next thing you know, you have been on the phone with him for a few hours. When you realize this, you insist that you have to get off the phone. But by this time, you have sacrificed your precious study time. And, not only is he not concerned about your setback he doesn't care enough about tomorrow's test to study himself.

It is a woman's nature to be nurturing, and there's nothing wrong with that. However, too often young women sacrifice time, plans, energy and resources in an effort to keep their boyfriends happy. If you ask many older women, they'll tell you they have put themselves last on so many occasions that they don't know how to put themselves first anymore. Remember, **start off the way you want to end up** with others, and with yourself.

Relationship scorecard

If you're open to dating someone but you are mainly focusing on getting yourself together academically and socially so that you can be on track to fulfill your dreams, that's great! Some young women have a real "chilled" attitude when it comes to guys because, right now, they are laying the foundation for their future and don't want the distractions that come with dating and being in a relationship. Be assured: This is OK.

Perhaps you are trying to establish a relationship, and no matter how hard you try, some guys are simply not relationship material right now. Truthfully, some may never be. One important lesson is to learn that a person can be no more to you than he can be to himself. This applies to you as well. Both of you can only be who you can be. This is real talk. So, stop trying to make him be who you want him to be. It's only going to frustrate you, and drive him away, making this is a lose-lose strategy.

This is not to say that some of your more positive attributes won't rub off on him, or his on you. Any positive influence someone can have on another person's life is a good thing. However, you shouldn't expect someone to be the person you want them to be simply because it's what YOU want. That's like trying to make an apple become a banana, which is totally unrealistic. If you're attracted to a guy for WHO HE IS, why are you expecting him to become a different person just because he is with you? If he chooses to change, that's one thing. But, if you're trying to make him change to fit your expectations you're being unreasonable, and may end up getting your feelings hurt when he decides he can't take the stress of trying to meet your expectations anymore.

Lesson 14

REALITY TV IS NOT YOUR REALITY

The art of being lady-like has been overtaken by the new bold behaviors inspired, in part, by what is promoted on reality TV programs. But reality TV is not realistic. It is manipulated entertainment. In spite of this, many real-world young ladies have taken on aspects of reality television celebrities popularized through their outrageous TV behavior. You know the women I'm talking about—the ones screaming, cussing, pulling-out hair and trying to make sure everyone knows how tough they are. No matter what's going on, they can handle the situation in two minutes.

I'm not knocking this type of program, if that's what you are into. However, I do want to remind those of you who are into reality TV programs that YOU ARE WATCHING TV! That means most of it isn't real. It's obvious that what is being aired has already happened, but what's not obvious is how much of it has been staged. How many of the arguments and disagreements are part of a pretend drama that has been hyped up for the sake of ratings? And, even if all the drama is real, the people involved are GETTING PAID! People who act like that in the real world just have one problem after another, and all their dramatic performances earn them nothing.

Some of you may be impressed by what you see on these programs, and may be influenced by reality TV celebrity behavior. If so, while you may think being a bit *cray-cray* is working in the moment, and you have your "crew" cheering you on, and everyone is talking about how you put whomever in "check," a lot of people—specifically young men—are turned off by it, whether they tell you that or not. I listen to guys all the time who talk about how far some young women will go to get their way, prove their point, or try to solve their problems, many times with an audience of their own. When you think about it, how many reality TV programs feature men yelling and screaming? You're right, there aren't any. Hmmmmmm. ...

What's really sad is to see young women attempting to solve their real-world situations using reality TV problem-solving techniques. While you think you're getting your point across, a lot of people are doing the **SMH** while they are watching. And, if your personal reality TV moment appears on YouTube with several likes, or you attract a lot of followers to your various forms of social media, it still does not make you a star. It makes you someone who is willing to risk your reputation for a moment of attention. And if you keep acting that way, as you grow older, you may find yourself suffering a shortage of friends and opportunities because most progressive people can't afford to be associated with people who lack impulse control.

The Angry Young Woman syndrome vs. being a Grateful Young Woman

In an earlier lesson, I asked if you know any mature women who are angry and bitter, for whatever reason. Many of you probably know of a woman who fits this description. But look around you. Do you know anyone your age who has the same tendencies? Do you know any angry, bitter, *young* women? Well I do, and there is nothing attractive about them. They look angry, they never speak in a pleasant tone and they are really LOUD. Like everyone else, they want to be loved by someone. Yet they make loving them very difficult. After a while, even if a young man is attracted to someone like this at first, he becomes exhausted from having to expend so much energy to do his part to keep the relationship alive. Eventually, battle-worn, he simply gives up.

I recall a young couple that had this challenge. The young man told me his girlfriend was always complaining, and was super-difficult to get along with. She would argue with him about everything, and most of the time he would just sit and look at her because he didn't know what else to do. Now, he was no saint either. But he really did care about her and tried his best to deal with her attitude even though she never seemed grateful. No matter what he did for her, he said she didn't bother to tell him "thank you," not even once.

I asked him why he continued to be involved with her, and he said that he really liked her, and that she had a lot to deal with in her personal life. But he was tired of the mistreatment, so I suggested that a relationship only works when both parties are trying to make it work. I added that if he wasn't happy, then he needed to make a decision. Shortly after that, the couple broke up. Later, I began to notice that whenever I saw him he looked much happier. His ex-girlfriend, on the other hand, continued to be angry and didn't seem to have a clue as to why he no longer wanted to be with her. *SMH*.

This situation shows the importance of courtesy and kindness. If a guy does something nice for you, please say thank you. Gratitude is the cornerstone of any healthy relationship. Because so many people have a sense of entitlement, they are ungrateful. When they receive a gift or someone does them a favor, they see no need to express their appreciation. Saying "thank you" seems to be a dying practice. It is up to you to resurrect it.

No one should be taken for granted, and everyone likes to be acknowledged for what they've done. It doesn't take much effort to do this in person or in a text message. Since many of you spend so much time posting on social media, what about publicly expressing your gratitude to the person who has shown you kindness? A simple "thank you" can go a long way.

I remember a young man who liked a very attractive young woman, and she knew it. He constantly tried to impress her by doing nice things for her. For example, he would hold the door open for her and carry her books. When he could afford it, he would even buy her simple snacks like chips and beverages. Of course, none of this was enough for her. She had a very strong sense of entitlement, and believed that whatever he did for her he was SUPPOSED to do if he wanted her attention. As far as I know, she never thanked him for anything.

After a while, he became annoyed and began to focus on someone who had a more loving spirit. As for the first young lady, she ended up dating a young man who only wanted to be with her for her looks. He neglected her and treated her worse than she had treated the guy who was once so into her.

Guys don't like being disrespected any more than you do. They like it when the young women they care about notices that they're trying to be good to them. They want to contribute to their girlfriend's happiness. This is a strong attribute for any young man to have, but it needs to be valued.

Lesson 15

IS YOUR LIFE AN OPEN BOOK?

What does it mean to have a mystique? A mystique is an aura of mystery. It creates an air of unpredictability. Because many young men like challenges, they are intrigued by young ladies who have a mystique, even if they don't know what it is!

Have you ever liked a young man who seemed to really be into you in the beginning, but became distant after a while for no apparent reason? Well, sometimes it's because you don't have a mystique. Several young men I have talked to have said that they like it when they have to figure certain things out about you; they find this captivating. It may be the depth of a comment you make which they need to interpret. (Guys like to analyze things.) It may be that they have to work a bit harder at times to know what is on your mind because you don't announce your every thought. Sometimes it can be your spontaneity, because it catches them off-guard. All these things keep them guessing, which keeps their interest in you alive.

A mystique is something you develop when you're confident. When you feel good about yourself, you're not always looking for someone to validate you. You're not arrogant, but you are sure of yourself. You're comfortable in your skin and able to be your authentic self. When you know who you are and believe in yourself with certainty, you are on your way to developing a mystique.

To find out if you have a mystique, take the **MYSTIQUE TEST**. Score each statement based on how it applies to you.

If your response is	Score
Always	1
Often	4
Seldom	7
Never	10

1. When _____ sends me an instant message or text message, I ALWAYS respond right away.

2. When he FaceTimes me, I answer every time.

3. If he asks me at the last minute to go somewhere with him—whether I have plans or not—I drop everything I'm doing so I can spend time with him.

4. I usually let him know all my daily plans.

5. If he and I have a disagreement, I usually act upset so he will know how I feel.

6. I have become distant from most of my friends because I'm in a relationship with him.

7. I always let him know that I'm available whenever he wants to spend time with me.

8. When I am getting dressed to see him, I make a point of always wearing my sexiest, sometimes revealing outfits to remind him of "what he has."

9. I always share all my thoughts with him; I tell him everything that's on my mind.

10. Even when there are things that I really want to do, if he calls me while I'm having fun of my own I usually stop whatever I'm doing to talk to him, or try to find my way to him if he wants to see me.

If you scored,

75 to 100	Congratulations! You have mystique. You keep him guessing.
50 to 74	Your mystique is evolving. With proper focus, it will develop over time.
10 to 49	You don't have much mystique. If you keep getting involved with guys who mistreat and disrespect you, re-evaluate your actions. Your life is an open book; easy to read and manipulate.

Let's analyze the Mystique Test to understand the significance of each item.

1 and 2. If you always respond to each text message or FaceTime contact right away, this can give the impression that you don't have anything going on in your life and that you are looking for this guy to be the reason you breathe. While a guy may appreciate your responsiveness on one level, a lot of them have told me they find it strange if a young lady always has so much availability and time. If you don't respond right away, they become more curious about you and what you're doing.

3. Nothing screams to your guy "You are my everything" and "I have nothing to do but be with you" more than dropping everything you are doing. At first, he may appreciate the fact that you are all-in and willing to do whatever it takes to be with him. But after a while, your availability may become so predictable that he loses interest. For some guys it can even turn into the "Watch, man, if I call her now I bet she'll drop everything for me" game. Spending quality time is one thing, but dropping whatever you're doing just for him may cause you to establish an unhealthy pattern that can cause problems for you as time goes on.

4. Why do you feel the need to give your guy a play-by-play of your day? This diminishes your ability to seem spontaneous. It may seem thoughtful early in your relationship, but after a while it can make you sound like you plan everything. Of course, you're telling him your every move for a few reasons: First, you are trying to function like a partner in a relationship by sharing your plans, but second, you really want him to know what's happening on your end so he will know when you will be available to spend time with him. Then you become disappointed if he doesn't try to schedule some form of contact with you. Also, most guys will rarely always provide a moment-to-moment accounting of their daily plans for you. A lot of times, even if you ask them, they won't offer many specifics, simply because they don't function that way. So, share your plans sometimes, especially plans you know he'd be interested in, but don't sound like a scheduler all the time.

5. Not letting a guy know that you're mad at him can be hard, especially if you're really mad at him. But sometimes the things he does to upset you aren't worth being mad about. Sometimes when a guy has had enough of being involved he will deliberately make you mad to push you away, which I will talk to you about later. Sometimes he is just being who he is. Either way, it will be in your best interest to just stay cool. The thing is, when a guy knows you're mad, he's expecting you to act like it. He's prepared for you to do whatever you do when he's frustrated you, and he's prepared for your reaction. So, sometime, use some reverse psychology, BE COOL and don't act mad! He'll be so confused he won't know what's going on.

6. Good friends are hard to come by, so don't drop them for any guy. Keep a balance and keep your friendships alive. Never make any guy your universe. Have a life of your own.

7. Don't let your guy know that you're always available. You're young, and have your own ambitions and goals. Value them. If you have something else planned to do that will give your life meaning, let him know that. He should respect that, and be interested.

8. Sometimes less is more. Everything you wear doesn't have to be super-short or super-low-cut. What you wear sends a signal about who you are. Besides, sometimes a chic, less revealing outfit can make you look classy. Nothing says "mystique" more than a touch of class.

9. STOP TALKING SO MUCH!!! I don't know how else to say this. First, most guys don't listen as much as women think they do. So, sharing your every thought with your guy will cause him to tune you out. A lot of times when you think you're talking to him you are actually talking at him. The conversation isn't about the two of you, it's really all about you. Second, stop broadcasting every detail that's on your mind. Believe it or not, a guy can feel indirectly pressured to fit into whatever grand life plan you may have for yourself. Sometimes he will simply smile while you're talking because he doesn't want you to think he's not paying attention because then you'll get mad, and he'll have to deal with your attitude. Sometimes he really doesn't know what to say, which, of course, also makes you mad. So, for him, having to listen to too much talking and not knowing what to do, or say, is a losing proposition.

I know what you may be thinking now: "But he listens to his friends. Why doesn't he want to listen to me?" Talking and listening to his boys is different. They have a language and understanding of life that is all their own. Allow him to have these connections.

Or you may be thinking: "I just sent him this text message with all these good details and things I'm really interested in, and he just sends back *OK* or *Fine*. Doesn't he care?" Well, give him room. Maybe what he's thinking about what you wrote is that it would be better to talk about it, one part at time, face to face, instead of sending you some large complicated text in return.

10. Most guys who are fairly smart have an idea when they are being manipulated. So, if you frequently feel the need to give him your daily schedule it may seem like that's your way of trying to get him to volunteer to be added to your calendar. So, let him ask you when he can see or talk to you, or be direct and let him know when you are free.

Don't forget, we're talking about having a mystique. If you're having fun with your friends, have fun with your friends. If he calls, you don't have to say anything more than "Hey, Babe! I'm out with my girls at the (movies, mall, whatever), but I promise to call you as soon as I'm free. Miss you! Talk to you later." END OF CONVERSATION! You don't need to spend a lot of time talking to him when you're with your friends.

You need to have power moves. A power move doesn't put you in control of the relationship, it keeps you in control of YOURSELF! Just think about it: When he doesn't want to talk to you, does he? When he wants to hang out with his friends, does he ask you if it's OK? Of course not! He is doing what he wants, when he wants, because he knows that whenever he does reach out to you will immediately fall back into the role of being the good predictable girlfriend.

I know a young lady who has a mystique, and she probably doesn't know she has one. She has been dating a very nice young man for close to two years, and she knows how to get his attention. Sometimes she is playful with him, and sometimes she is distant. When she is slightly distant, it isn't necessarily because she's upset with him. It's because she needs HER space. When she is being reserved, he gives her his full attention because he can't really tell what's on her mind. I have watched him go out of his way to ask her if she is OK, and she responds only by saying "I'm fine." The silence keeps him guessing. She has never been one to discuss her thoughts with many people and post everything that's on her mind on social media. And she's not one to play games. So, it isn't as though she's trying to get back at her boyfriend for anything he may or may not have done. She moves gracefully, and with a great deal of confidence. And he's usually not far behind almost every step of the way.

Is her relationship with her boyfriend perfect? Not at all. She and her guy have broken up and gotten back together a few times. But when they were not together, she handled it. A person who wasn't aware that they weren't together would never have known based on how she carried herself. And, when she and her boyfriend weren't together, he could easily have taken advantage of their separation and pursued someone else. Not only is he a nice guy, he's good-looking, too! But he is really into her, and even though they may frustrate each other at times, her mystique keeps him intrigued.

A few young ladies shared with me that their boyfriends have hit them with the 'L' word (love), which was totally unexpected and caught them by surprise. They each liked their boyfriends a lot but didn't necessarily feel the same way, at least not yet; they enjoyed their relationships but were more focused on getting themselves together. I asked them how they reacted to what their boyfriends said, and they told me they stalled giving a response long enough to ask a few of their close friends for advice about what they should do. Some were advised to tell their guys they feel the same way because it wouldn't be nice to hurt their feelings, especially when "A good man is hard to find." But two of these young women were super-smart, and independent- thinkers with **power moves**. They decided to be honest and tell the truth.

So many young women are so anxious to hear "I love you" they automatically respond by saying the same thing, whether they really feel this way or not. No relationship can stand on a foundation of dishonesty. Remember, during the lesson on communication being a two-way street, I mentioned the importance of transparency. These young ladies were quick to communicate their feelings, leaving no room for anyone to have to play the guessing game. And, how empowering it is to be honest without fear of whether your guy will leave you if you don't tell him what he wants to hear! These young women didn't feel they were taking a risk because if any of their guys walked away, they would have been fine because they feel good within themselves. They would rather be honest, first with themselves, then with their guys. They refused to be dishonest to keep someone around just to avoid being alone. When you are self-confident, power moves are not difficult to make.

Having a mystique is helpful in committed, long-term relationships as well. I know you're not ready for this phase of your life, but if you practice developing and maintaining a mystique now, it can stay with you into the future. For example, when a couple has been dating for an extended period of time, or have been married for a few years or longer, it's easy to become so comfortable and relaxed that one partner begins taking the other one for granted. The original points of attraction—whatever they were—have faded away. On this point, here's some old-school wisdom for you at an early age: Whatever you do to attract someone, you must do to keep them.

So, don't forget to keep your mystique.

If my score indicates that I don't have a mystique, how do I get one?

If your score reveals that you don't have a mystique, don't panic; it only means that you may have some self-work to do. For instance, if you are being honest with yourself, do you talk too much? Are you sharing things about yourself that are no one's business? Do you wear clothes that are too revealing? Do you allow yourself to be too accessible to others? Only you know the answers to these questions.

Cultivating a mystique requires self-honesty. Throughout your life there will be times when you will have to have candid conversations with yourself if you want to further your self- development. Until you learn to face yourself, developing a mystique- and other things—will continue to be a mystery.

"But he loves me..."

A word of caution: If you're dealing with a guy who becomes angry when he cannot reach you, or always has to know where you are and what you're doing, having a mystique is not the issue. The issue is that you're dealing with someone who likely has aggressive tendencies. This behavior is not "cute." Please stop telling yourself that "he's just being protective" or "he's just doing it because he loves me." Let me tell you right now that love is not controlling, nor is it abusive or aggressive. This type of behavior can escalate and lead to problems of serious abuse.

What guys have to say about young women with a mystique

Guys like the element of surprise. They like piecing things together. They like the hunt. Think about it. The activities many young men enjoy most are video games, action movies and sports—all of which involve an aspect of unpredictability. If they could always anticipate the next move with any of these activities they would probably hurry off to do something else.

OK, now that you have been introduced to mystique, I need to add a few words of caution. Creating a mystique is bit like walking on a tightrope. There is a fine line between having it and forcing guys to have to become psychic to read your mind. Don't forget the earlier lesson dealing with communication, where guys stated very clearly that they don't like having to always play the guessing game to find out what's on your mind. Be intriguing but don't overdo it. Find the right sharing balance between going overboard and being too closed. Just keep working at it. Once you develop your mystique you will find it to be a valuable asset. When a guy compares you to other young women—which he is likely to do—your mystique will help you stand above all others.

Lesson 16

HEAR WHAT HE SAYS, WATCH WHAT HE DOES

It doesn't matter how much a guy may tell you he cares about you, that you are his one and only, blah, blah, blah, if he doesn't show it. Or have a chance to. If you are busy doing everything for both of you, you won't be able to observe what he is contributing to the relationship.

Allow him to have an active role. Encourage him to suggest where to go on the weekend. Let him arrange the transportation, or pick you up when you're going out. Invite him to meet people who are significant in your life. If he shies away from that, it's a red flag. If he talks to you about the people who are important to him but you are never introduced to them, that's a huge red flag! This doesn't mean there has to be a formal family introduction around the dinner table. However, he should be interested enough to want to know more about you—and this includes meeting the people who matter to you. He should want you to know the people who matter to him as well. This will give both of you a glimpse into each other's worlds, and provide insight into your backgrounds, your values and the type of person each of you are.

When you are with him in public, does he act like he's with you, or does he seem distant like you're not significant? Does he hold the door open for you? When you're ordering at a restaurant, is he courteous by allowing you to order first?

Is he treating you as an equal? Is he being an equal part of the relationship? Just like communication, relationships are like a two-way street.

Lesson 17

DON'T GET TRAPPED WITH SOCIAL MEDIA AND EXPLICIT FLICKS

What is your social media image? It is appropriate? What types of pictures do you post? Do you make matters public that should be kept private? What are you telling the world about who you are?

Too many young women have very poor social media practices. Many young men have poor practices too, but we already have had a discussion about society's unfair double standards. Certain behaviors impact young women in ways that do not affect young men, at least to the same extent. That's just the way it is. So when it comes to your presence on social media you have to be very careful about the image you convey. You may think you are living in the moment, but the long-term effects can be difficult to live down.

A few years ago, I was talking to a young man who was offering his opinion about some of the things young women were posting. During our conversation, he told me about "a serious THOT" who had posted some horribly "ratched" pictures of herself. As it happens, the young lady he was talking about was someone I knew. The photos he described were beyond belief; I couldn't believe this young lady was degrading herself like that.

So, of course, I had to say something to her about what I had been told. When I asked her about it, she was very surprised that I knew. The expression on her face changed from happy to embarrassment. Then she told me that she hadn't made the posts; someone had created a social media presence with her images. She insisted that she had nothing to do with what was happening and couldn't control it. The more she tried to persuade me that she was innocent, the less I believed her.

What was sad about this situation was that it didn't matter whether I believed her or not. Her reputation had been tarnished and the aftershock will follow her for years to come. Many young women are destroying their lives because of what they are posting on Instagram, Snapchat and Twitter. I have a QQ4U: What are you thinking????!!!!

Truthfully, I don't believe that many of you are thinking at all. You're just living in the moment, and you're not considering the consequences of your decisions. You may not believe what I am saying is a big deal, but trust me, it IS a big deal. I really need you to think about this topic. More and more colleges, employers, and professional organizations are scrutinizing prospective candidates' social media.

A few years ago, I attended a high school's Career Day, and listened to the presentation of a representative from Homeland Security who explained that there is no such thing as "deleting" images from **any** form of social media. Once you put yourself out there, you're out there. You can take information down, or try to clean it up, but you can't control or determine how far your image(s) may have traveled already. People have lost out on career opportunities because of their inappropriate presentations.

And, in terms of guys you might meet, a young man will look at someone like this as a "minute girl," because even if he is attracted to her, he won't be interested that long.

Here's the thing: As exciting as it might seem at the time—in fact, especially if it feels exciting to do it—DO NOT post anything in writing or any visual if you don't want it to be seen later by the public.

What guys say about explicit media posts

When I talked to the guys about this, they were rather to-the-point. For them, explicit media posts are in the ratched, rat, or THOT category. They are used to seeing posts of this nature, and aren't fazed by it as long as it's not being done by someone they have a serious interest in. They went on to add that "There are some guys who are into that sort of thing," so, I guess if you are dealing with a guy who does not care about how you look on your social media, it won't affect the way he views you. However, what about how others may perceive you … a college that you may want to attend, a prospective employer, or a guy you may find yourself attracted to down the line? Remember, once you put yourself out there like that, you can't take it back.

Some of you don't seem to be bothered by these references because, in your mind, these descriptions are about someone else, some THOT who put herself in a situation to be disrespected, which makes being disrespected **their** problem, because you're not that girl. And then your personal social media images surface.

I was recently riding in my car with my window down, enjoying a pleasant breeze on a sunny day. Everything was fine until I came to a stoplight and a car pulled up next to me that was blasting a song about "running a train on a #@!" I was so shocked at the lyrics that I forgot to get going when the light turned green.

Later, when I asked around about the song and the artist, several people told me there are a lot of songs that suggest treating women this way. Why would anyone think it's OK to write these lyrics and put them to music? Have these songs been produced for shock value, or do the people who recorded them really believe what they're saying? And, for the guys who listen to this music, what type of images flow through their minds when they're rapping along with the lyrics? If you have ever heard one of these songs, how did you react? Were you offended? Did you become upset? Did you have any reaction at all? Or did you just overlook what you were hearing by telling yourself that "it's just a song" without giving any thought to its implications?

You may not be the girl, or young woman, who has the over-the-top pictures on your sites. But what are you calling yourself on your social media? If you are listening to the music in question, are you taking those cues and referencing yourself in the same way? If the words you use to describe yourself are inappropriate or suggestive that's just as bad as having explicit photos. By giving yourself a degrading label, you are suggesting that because you don't respect yourself, you shouldn't be respected. Either way, you are imaging yourself in a way that may cost you.

Check yourself

Educational institutions and prospective employers scrutinize applicants' social media profiles for admissions or employment. What does your social media profile say about your character? Do you consider the implications—good or bad—of what you post?

Responses to social media posts can affect a person's self-esteem, especially if they are berated, insulted, taunted or bullied. But people cannot respond to posts that don't exist, so if you don't put yourself out there, no one will have anything harmful to say about you!

Be mindful that what may appear to be a positive response to a post can lull you into a sense of believing something about yourself that may not be true. Take time to assess your social media image.

Social Media Profile Self-check

YOUR IDENTIY AND PERONAL BRAND

- What is your name on your social media?
- If you are not using your name, what statement does it make about you and your character?
- Based on your personal brand- how you represent yourself- would you hire yourself, write yourself a letter of

recommendation, or introduce yourself to a nice guy who is looking for a young woman of quality?
- What type of identity are you trying to create? Why?

YOUR POSTING STRATEGY
- What inspires you to post?
- How often do you post?
- Are your posts reactive? In other words, do you think about what you post in advance- are you logical- or do typical respond emotionally?
- Do you post personal images? If so, what types of pictures of yourself do you post?
- What types of posts do you respond to? What attracts you to these types of posts? Do you participate in social media bullying, insults, or involve yourself in matters that are none of your concern?

CONSIDER YOUR LAST 10 POSTS
- How many of your posts were positive?
- In response to someone's post, did you offer encouraging, uplifting advice or suggestions?
- How many of your posts were negative?
- Did you instigate, or give your opinion to someone that could potentially lead to confusion, drama, or harm?
- How many were personal?
- How many were explicit?
- How many have included inappropriate language?

YOUR EXPECTATIONS
- Do you solicit responses for personal matters? If so why, and what type of responses are you expecting?
- Do you respond to others looking for advice? If so, are you offering the quality of advice you would want someone to give you?
- Are you concerned about the number of likes you receive?

YOUR FOLLOWERS
- How many followers do you have?
- Are you concerned about the number of 'likes' you receive, or the number of responses you receive to your posts? If so, why does this matter to you?
- Do you and your follow share qualities? What do you have in common with them?
- Do you feel responsible to those who follow you? Why, or why not?

THE IMPACT
- What will a prospective college or employer learn about you based on what you post?
- Do you ever post comments that can cost you your career, job, friendship, or relationship?
- Do you ever take time to think about the impact of what you post before you post it, or do you prefer to say what you have to say, and deal with the consequences later?
- Are you ever concerned about the potential consequences of your posts, or do you think that whatever happens as a result of what you post is simply not your problem?

Take responsibility for your personal brand. Control your image. Don't make yourself the victim of explicit neediness. Be careful about what you post. Don't get trapped.

Lesson 18

YOU MUST BE INTO CRYIN' IF YOU BELIEVE HIS LYIN'

In an earlier lesson, we covered the importance of effective communication. I suggested that when you're talking to your guy that you should listen to what he has to say about whatever concerns you may have (without over-the-top emotion). I encouraged you to observe his body language during face-to-face discussions so that you could observe his level of engagement. I also told you to pay attention to what he says, and what he doesn't say. Hopefully you found that to be sound advice.

However, if you are dealing with a guy who is constantly making excuses about everything, and every time you ask him the same question two or three different ways, he gives you a different answer each time, he is probably not being honest with you. In many cases, your intuition is screaming at you that he's lying about something, but you excuse it away and accept what he says. Sometimes, you actually catch him in a lie, but you give him opportunities to explain and talk his way out of it. When you discover that he has been dishonest with you on multiple occasions, you become angry, and cry. What's up with that?

I think you must be into cryin' if you believe his lyin'! Why put yourself through that agony? Why try to figure out how to get the password to his phone or his Snapchat account so you can go through his messages to find out how many times he has lied to you? That's entirely too much work.

Why would you want to continue a relationship with someone who is being dishonest? I mean, really? How do you justify that? What internal dialogue are you having that allows you to keep dealing with someone who is letting you know who he is? Why don't you believe what he is showing you? Remember, if it walks like a duck, and it talks like a duck, it's a duck!

I know a few college freshman couples who have been together since high school, and the current scenarios are similar with all of them. Although they have been with each other for a while, when I say they were together I mean the young ladies were together with the guys, but their guys were together with them plus a few other young ladies. Still, the ladies said they loved their long-time guys. *SMH*. They would do whatever was necessary to keep them.

Here's a true story to learn from. I talked to a young man in high school on multiple occasions and told him he wasn't ready for a committed relationship. He agreed! But he really liked his girlfriend and decided that he was going to make the necessary changes to keep her.

Fast forward to their college years. They were still a couple, and he had cut back on his dealings with other young ladies. But he still wasn't quite there yet. And because she knew that, she didn't trust him. She was constantly checking to see where he was, what he was doing and where he was going. She checked his phone for evidence that he had been seeing someone other than her. When I asked her why she continued to deal with him, she said she still loved him. SMH.

As I talked to other young ladies who were hanging on to their relationships by a thread, they loved their boos, too. I had to ask each of them, "Boo, who?"

Recently a young woman came to talk to me about her ex-boyfriend, who was dating someone else yet showing interest in her again. He was calling and texting her, and constantly trying to engage her in conversation. She felt torn because while she still found him attractive she didn't want to create problems between him and his new girlfriend. My suggestion to her was to distance herself from the young man. But he kept flirting with her, which of course led to his new girlfriend finding out.

THINK ABOUT IT...

What do you think happened next?

Of course the girlfriend began asking her boyfriend what was going on, and he denied knowing what she was talking about, and said that he was the victim because she was "falsely accusing" him, and that if she couldn't trust him, there was no reason to be in a relationship anymore. His girlfriend believed him and immediately became angry at his ex-girlfriend. She proceeded to attack the ex-girlfriend, who hadn't done anything more than hold out hope.

What is really interesting is how, in this situation and many similar to it, the girlfriend is quick believe her boyfriend and attack the other woman.

First, if you are dealing with a guy who has a history of being a player, don't be eager to believe everything he says. Calm down long enough to process the situation before you react. What is the evidence that you have? Is dealing with the possible truth that your guy is heavily flirting with his ex so painful that you would rather attack an innocent young woman than address your concerns to him? Even if he isn't the player type, if he is still attracted to his former girlfriend, don't you want to know the truth about where you stand with him? And, if he is trying to involve himself with someone else, he is fully aware of what he is doing. He's the person you should be upset with first, because no matter what the other young woman has said or done, he could have reminded her that he is with you and walked away.

When guys are allowed to play dumb about their role in creating this type of situation, they will take the opportunity and run with it, if you allow it. After all, who wants to get busted for having the best of both worlds? The old-school expression for this is wanting to have your cake and eat it, too. If you maintain your standards and value yourself, he will be forced to make a decision about whether he wants to risk losing you.

However, if you're dealing with a guy and you know he's lying to you, *SMH*. I have nothing else to say.

Lesson 19

DON'T I KNOW YOU FROM SOMEWHERE? DATING THE SAME TYPE OVER AND OVER

In an earlier lesson, you were asked to think about what characteristics you look for in a guy, and what you would prefer not to deal with. I'm asking you again to give thought to what attracts you to a young man.

It's not unusual to be attracted to someone because of the way he looks. A lot of women are attracted to a specific type. It could be because of popularity, or because he is "so sexy." Maybe you are into guys who are athletic, rappers, or poets. Do you have a thing for guys who have a bad boy reputation? Are you attracted to guys who are considerate, thoughtful, respectful, and caring? Or are you into guys who pay attention to you when most others don't?

Well, consider this: Whatever the thing is that first attracts you to someone can blind you to who he really is. You're so caught-up with how you *feel* when you're with him, or simply think about him, that you don't pay attention to what may be glaring warning signs.

How many of you have a friend who has been mistreated by every guy she has ever dealt with? Have you wondered why the same scenario captures her life over and over again? Eventually, many young women like this begin to feel bad about themselves and question their self-worth. What they should do instead is look at what they're attracted to in a guy, and try to understand the source of that attraction.

We talked earlier about young women who are looking for a daddy in the guys they date. This is a really big deal, and can be a really big problem. If you're looking for the guy because you're trying to fill a void, you won't be picking up on a guy who will be your trusted **friend** who shares your values and is willing to support you and appreciate the support you're offering him.

Dating is a trial-and-error process for everyone. Most people date a few people before they discover who is best for them, and how to make the relationship work. The thing is that whatever draws someone to you or draws you to them needs to be examined so that you are not continually becoming involved with the type of guy who is not the right fit for you. Again, *you need to assess before you become a mess*. But in this instance, the person you need to assess is yourself.

STOP, LOOK, AND LISTEN!!!

Lesson 20

DRAMA ADDICTS

Do you know people who seem to have their own personal clouds of drama that follow them everywhere they go? With them, nothing is simple and easy. They seem to be addicted to drama, and may not be able to function without it. People like this ALWAYS have a situation that needs to be resolved. Either they're not getting along with someone, they're mad at someone, someone is mad at them, they have just been put out of the house, they're arguing with their parents, they don't have bus fare, their car is down—the list goes on and on. They always have an issue with someone or something. Even the smallest thing can become a huge problem for such people. It's almost as if the drama is part of their identity.

If you're not careful, they will pull you into their world over and over again.

A problem with people who thrive on drama is that you can't get them to see that they often either create it or fuel it—they keep it going when the situation should have been over with long ago. Sometimes the situations they find themselves in are due to faulty decision-making and their inability to **assess so they won't be a mess**. Sometimes their dramatic tendencies stem from their need for attention, and sometimes the drama is the result of behavior learned from their environment. In any case, it has become part of who they are. And they are never satisfied unless others are caught up in their drama with them.

I know a young lady who always has some sort of drama going on. She always has a problem with a teacher, a "friend," or someone. Here's an example: She had been in a relationship with a young man and it had come to an end, but they were on good terms with each other. It wasn't a bitter breakup; she and he had agreed that it just wasn't working for them anymore. She moved on and met someone else who seemed very interested in her, and she seemed happy.

All was well until her ex decided that he wanted to pursue someone else. As soon as that happened, she went into attack mode and began spreading horrible rumors about his new young lady, even though she didn't know anything about her. She even persuaded her friends that they shouldn't like this young lady, either. In a matter of days, she and her team of *haters* were on a mission to break her ex and his new girl apart, even though she herself had someone new. Why do you think she would she take so much time away from her own life to disrupt someone else's?

And, you may ask, what about her new boo? Well, all that drama made him lose interest and he moved on to someone else.

Like you, I was a bit curious about why this young lady allowed her personal cloud of drama to disrupt her progress. But when I met her mother, many of my questions were answered. It was obvious that the young lady's behaviors had been passed on to her. I'm not *throwing shade* about her mom. I'm simply stating a fact. Her mom was loudly and publicly discussing her own personal business about what someone had done that she didn't like, how she was going to deal with the situation, and how she had called her "girl" to tell her what was going on. The whole time she was talking I was thinking to myself "OMG ... seriously? No one cares about your drama." At that moment, she should have been much more concerned about the trouble her daughter was having in school. But, in that moment, it was apparent that she was a source of her daughter's drama-queen behavior. And, based on her comments about her own situation, she definitely had a lot more drama to give.

If you tend to be a drama queen, you really need to let it go. I have witnessed young ladies being extra when it comes to how they react to a variety of scenarios involving their boyfriends.

She said, she said, she said, he said, he said, she said...

How many times have you known breakups or a couple's problems to occur because someone said something to someone about something, which was none of their business to begin with? There are some people who ALWAYS seem to do these three things consistently: get into your business, misinterpret it, and spread it. Of course, you can make that worse by telling them everything you have going on. And, while I totally understand your need to talk to your girls sometimes, some of you are not **assessing** the personalities of some of the people in your circle.

Let me put it another way: You may not be a drama queen yourself, but you share your business with people who are. It doesn't matter how long you may have known this person, or how close you may be to them. If they are drama addicts, then you will become their victim and have to constantly put out the fires they start. Even if their intentions are good and they believe they are helping or protecting you, their blow-it-up approach to problem-solving ultimately creates problems for you. The next thing you know, your relationship is in jeopardy, and while you're trying to repair it, your business continues to leak.

Perhaps you know someone who has been involved with the following scenario: A young lady and her guy are having the ups and downs like any couple trying to navigate a relationship. At some point, the young lady shares a few details with a friend about some challenges she's having with her boyfriend. The friend that she tells can't contain herself. She's so excited to know something that no one else knows that she embellishes the story by putting her personal spin on it as she tells one of her "trusted" friends who tells someone else who then tells the young lady's boyfriend.

Well, you know what happens next. He gets upset with his girlfriend for over-sharing and putting their private business into the streets. The girlfriend gets angry at her friend for revealing something she had told her in confidence, and her friend responds by getting angry at her. Are you following this? The bottom line is that the person who retold the confidential story is a drama addict and she pulled everyone else into the chaos.

THINK ABOUT IT

Drama queen check

1. Do you feel the need to argue with your boyfriend almost all the time?
2. Do you over-react if you think another girl likes him and is trying to get his attention even if he is not responding to her advances?
3. Do you rely on your "girls" to be part of your look-out crew to keep you informed about what your boyfriend may be doing or saying when you're not with him?
4. If he does something that you don't like, do you constantly throw his mistake into his face?
5. When you're mad at him, do you post ANY of your feelings and personal business about it on social media

Drama kings!

Typically, when you think about someone who is constantly involved with some type of drama, a female comes to mind. I couldn't end this discussion about drama addicts without adding that men can be addicted to drama, too. The addiction is not determined by gender; instead, it is driven by a person's seeming attraction, even need, to be in the eye of the storm of confusion. Among some, there is the perception that young men don't create drama, but this couldn't be further from the truth.

I have known several young men who lived dramatic lives. They kept everyone in their circle on edge because they seemed to have a chip on their shoulder everywhere they went. They constantly had disagreements with people; they needed to be talked out of getting into bad situations. Or they were being rescued from bad situations they had already created. If a drama king has a girlfriend, she is almost always pulled into the quicksand with him.

I'm mentioning this to you because if you are not drama-prone yourself, you may want to avoid dealing with a young man who is. IT IS NOT YOUR RESPONSIBILITY TO FIX HIM, OR SAVE HIM!!!! Do you want a boyfriend, or a project? A young man who constantly needs to be calmed down or discouraged from putting himself in harm's way can become an energy drain. And, if he is constantly dealing with drama, when will there be time for him to really get into you?

What guys have to say about drama addicts

The guys I talked to said that some of you are really over-the-top drama queens. They added that constantly having to deal with your dramatic ways is exhausting, because in many cases it isn't even necessary. They don't like dealing with your constant loud talking, or constant arguing. If you have a problem with something they may or may not be doing, talk with them (and listen). All the extreme behavior becomes a turn-off over time.

Some of you may say, "He knew I was that way when we met, so why should I have to change?" Well, has it ever occurred to you that he may have thought he could tolerate your behavior but now is having second thoughts? And has it ever occurred to you that perhaps that over-the-top behavior may be turning a lot of people off? Do you really think being this way is making you more attractive to others? How is it helping you? What are you gaining from it? Is it improving the quality of your life? If you're shrugging your shoulders and thinking "That's the way I am," think again and pay close attention to how long your relationships last. That may help you get a clue.

The young men I talked to admitted that some guys really are drama kings—and they may appeal to some of you, on some level. Just remember that drama attracts drama, and sometimes you can get trapped in a vicious cycle of mishaps or unfortunate events that never seem to end. It's like being on a drama ferris wheel.

So, whether you are a drama queen or someone who is dealing with a drama king, pay attention to how much this confusion is affecting your schoolwork, your relationship and your family. You can't control anyone but yourself, so be accountable for your behavior, and walk away from anyone who can't control his.

How do you resolve conflicts?

One trait that most drama addicts seem to have in common is the inability to solve problems without some form of public display. Whether it's causing a loud scene in public or on social media, drama addicts seem to have a tendency for letting the world know they have a problem, and that they are going to "handle" the problem. In many instances, what they consider to be a resolution to whatever the problem may be doesn't resolve the problem at all. It only creates more drama.

Of course, drama addicts are not the only ones who need to work on developing better conflict resolution skills. How do you resolve conflicts? Do you talk it out, or do you curse it out, and shout it out? Do you hurl insults? Do you blast people and add fuel to the fire via social media? If any of these approaches describe your efforts, perhaps you need to employ a new technique because all of the above are beneath you.

On several occasions, I have talked to young women during a heated moment who are expressing their intentions to "slap him" or "beat her." Some of them will call their posse to get them on board to launch an attack at the first opportunity when they feel they have been wronged. What's the expression? "They've got me messed up!" Well, in that moment you may feel like messin' someone up, but I would like you to consider resolving conflicts in a nonviolent manner because the actions you think you should take will lead to consequences you won't want to face.

Most young men don't want to deal with someone who is always causing a scene. Of course, there are always exceptions. I just introduced the concept of *drama kings* to you. But people who are conflict-prone and always feel the need to make a scene have very brief relationships because they're too hard to deal with. In fact, they're exhausting.

This may sound crazy to you, but sometimes just having a conversation with someone to gain understanding and insight can be effective. Arguing your way through every issue simply doesn't work. A young man who used to go through this with his now ex-girlfriend endured her behavior for several months. After they had broken up, he asked me, "Why didn't you tell me she's crazy?" It wasn't my place to tell him that. But I'm glad he moved on to find someone more peaceful and lady-like.

Conflict resolution practice

Let's take a look at a few scenarios requiring conflict resolution. Following each one, explain how you would typically address the situation, and then give thought to another approach to solving the problem. You really need to be honest with yourself during this exercise. If you know your first response is what you would actually do, but probably not appropriate, write it down anyway. Do not write something first just because you feel it's the right thing to say. Be your true self! This is a great opportunity for you to look at some of your genuine thoughts on paper.

SCENARIO 1

You and your friend have been besties since the 9th grade. You two have shared and kept each other's secrets, and have supported each other through personal challenges. But now that you're in your senior year in high school, you're not as close as you used to be because you have matured and she hasn't. Now that you have a new set of friends, she feels betrayed and begins leaking some of your secrets to others, and it gets back to you. How would you handle this situation?

What I would probably do is...	A better resolution would be...
What would the outcome be?	What would the outcome be?

SCENARIO 2

You and a young man are very good friends. You have a few classes together and share study notes in class. You seek each other's advice when you're not sure how to handle a situation. Whenever anyone suggests that the two of you would make a cute couple, you explain that you are "just friends" and "he is more like a brother." Of course, you really do like him a lot, but accept your friendship status. At some point, it seems that he is becoming interested in you in a different way. At first you are hesitant, but because you have always had feelings for him, you become open to the possibility that he actually likes you. You both become more relaxed with each other, and before you know it you have really fallen for him. The problem is that he has met someone else that he is really into. He hasn't told you yet. However, right before you go to a class you share with him, a classmate tells you about posts and comments between him and the other girl on social media. How would you handle this situation?

What I would probably do is...	A better resolution would be...
What would the outcome be?	What would the outcome be?

SCENARIO 3

One afternoon, a friend of yours is showing you some Instagram posts in her phone. While she is scrolling through, you notice some pictures of her and your boyfriend. When you ask her about them, she explains that they were old photos from before the two of you got together. But the outfit he is wearing in the picture is one you helped him select when you were at a store a few weekends ago. How would you handle this situation?

What I would probably do is...	A better resolution would be...
What would the outcome be?	What would the outcome be?

No matter what a situation may be, you always have the power to exercise self-control. If you have the tendency to resolve conflicts with anger, you may become just like one of those angry, bitter women we discussed way back in Lesson 2. Some situations may require a direct response, but sometimes it might be better to just let things be. Learn to separate your emotions from the facts. You're capable, and smart. Keep a level head and get control of your emotions as you work through your conflicts.

What are your emotional triggers?

Another aspect of conflict resolution involves emotional triggers, the things that push your buttons and cause you to have a negative reaction. It can be something small, such as someone looking at you the wrong way, something a little bigger, like someone making unfavorable comments about you, or something really big, like someone touching you in an aggressive or inappropriate manner.

Sometimes you can agitate one of your triggers yourself. For example, if you have an internal dialogue—a conversation in your head that no one knows you are having—you can agitate one of your triggers all by yourself. You may see someone you don't like and spend hours thinking about what that person may have done or said to you, even if your encounter was weeks ago. The conversation you have with yourself might go something like this:

"There she is. Oooohhhhh ... I can't stand her! Just looking at her makes me sick. And look at what she is wearing. YOU'RE NOT CUTE! I don't know why they are over there talking to her. She gets on my nerves. And she better not come over here and say anything to me..."

And the dialogue within your head goes on and on and on. You walk around with an attitude for the next few hours all because you kept rewinding and playing the recording in your head. Until you can get past your thoughts, you snap at everyone around you and they have no idea why. When they ask you what's the matter, you don't want to talk about it. Even if you decide to share your thoughts, what do you say? You try to explain that "I am upset because I saw someone who made me mad about three weeks ago. I have not seen her since then and she didn't see me today, but if she had said anything to me I would have cussed her out." *Uh, yeah, I guess that might make sense.*

You continue to snap at everyone and take your frustrations out on the people who care about you because someone who didn't see you didn't give you the chance to tell them off. Well, whether the stimulus is internal or external, whatever sets you off is a trigger. You should identify your triggers so you can manage them.

Some of you might know someone who is a walking and talking trigger and celebrates her negative attitude. I have known several young women who seem to get a thrill from announcing "I know I have a bad attitude. People tell me that all of the time." Young women who make it clear to everyone that they have a bad attitude are almost looking for reasons to overreact to practically anything. It really seems to be more of a defense mechanism that prevents anyone from getting too close to them, or they are using this to get attention. Perhaps they have been hurt, or mistreated. Whatever the reason, everything in the world is a trigger for them. So, a young man may not approach someone who has this personality because unless he likes to argue—which most guys don't like to do—the relationship will be dead on arrival.

On the other hand, most people have triggers. There is nothing wrong with having them as long as you're capable of identifying and controlling them because, if you don't, it can lead to consequences, some of which may be irreparable.

Here's a scenario to consider. Let's say you're talking to one of your "girls" in the cafeteria during lunch. The two of you are excitedly discussing the coming weekend and your plans with your boyfriends. At the next table, a young woman who doesn't like you because you're dating her best friend's ex-boyfriend, and who is convinced that they broke up because of you, overhears your weekend plans. She then *throws shade* at you by saying, "Whatever she's planning to do will definitely be lame." In that moment, you are experiencing a potential trigger.

THINK ABOUT IT

How would you react?

This could play out in one of two ways. If you have the ability to exercise control, you will certainly become irritated but you will also consider the source, roll your eyes, take a deep breath, and continue the conversation with your friend. The young lady *throwing shade* has presented a trigger to you, but you are *over it* and won't waste any of your energy even looking in her direction. But, if you choose to react, you will allow your trigger to draw you into a situation that could lead to yelling, screaming, or more. And if you are a drama addict, any trigger is seeking an opportunity to turn you inside out so that it can be released into your drama addiction.

Poorly managed triggers can kill a relationship. I don't know how many young men have complained to me that they "are not psychic" and have no idea why you're upset about whatever is going on in your head. They also don't understand how it is that they could have said or done something to you today that actually triggered a thought in your head about something that happened six months ago. Guys' brains don't operate that way. They tend to deal with what is happening now, not yesterday. So, when you reach back in time to connect the past to the present because you haven't let something go, they have no idea how to respond.

Triggers can create problems not only with your boyfriend but with anyone you have a relationship with, whether family or friends. Most people who know you likely know your personality and are aware of those things that can set you off. I would like to discourage you from wearing your triggers like they are a badge of honor. Yes, I can hear some of you saying, "That's just the way I am." Well, if you choose to let your triggers control you, you're right, that's you. But if you keep letting your triggers dictate your life, I would like to know how that ends up working for you.

If you take the time to analyze the source of your triggers it might help you get a handle on them before they create an emotional eruption. As you are thinking about what they are, please also consider what some of the consequences have been when you have acted before thinking. What are your triggers? What are the things that cause emotional sparks to fly for you? List a few of them here, and what causes them to activate.

MY TRIGGERS ARE	THEY BECOME ACTIVE WHEN	THE CONSEQUENCES ARE
1.		
2.		
3.		
4.		
5.		

Having friendships and being in relationships with someone who is always on the emotional edge is extremely difficult. No one is really happy being around an emotional ticking time bomb. You have to handle your triggers; they shouldn't handle you.

Having triggers vs. being a trigger

I was talking to a young man the other day who was complaining about a young lady he likes who seems to take pleasure in taunting him to the point that he feels like becoming physical with her. He went on to say that he would never do such a thing because he has a sister himself, and he loves and respects his mother. But his comment made me think about times when a young woman has physically attacked a young man out of frustration with him or his behavior or has pushed a young man to the point where he lost it and responded to her forcefully. **It is never acceptable for a young man to aggressively put his hands on a young woman**. In Lesson 7 we discussed the possible ways for you to avoid abusive situations with a guy. However, I do want to make the point that **you should never hit a young man** and assume that he won't respond to you in the same way. Many guys know that your strength doesn't match theirs, and they will walk away from you. But some guys will be intolerant of you using them as a punching bag and may react by hitting you back. Again, I totally disagree with a response of this type. I am only saying that you can't hit a guy and assume that he will take it, and walk away. Not all young men have the discipline to ignore being attacked.

    I have talked to quite a few young men who have dated young women whose primary method of managing their frustration toward their boyfriends was rather aggressive. From what a few of the guys shared with me, their girlfriends sounded a bit "cray-cray" in the first place. Sometimes if her beauty is in her booty they are willing to forgive the crazy behavior. These guys generally had enough self-control to walk away when their girl started trippin.' But a few of them became fed up to the point that they totally snapped, and either pushed, hit or choked their girlfriend, or left them with an obvious sign of a physical encounter.

    It's one thing to **have** triggers, but it's another thing to **be** a trigger. If your guy frustrates you to the point where you feel the need to taunt or attack him, perhaps he's not the guy for you. And if you are honest with yourself, you may realize that your response to anyone who really frustrates you may evoke the same behavior. If this sounds like you, any decent guy is going to give up at some point and walk away. Healthy relationships don't lend themselves to being a trigger for anyone.

    Here's another scenario to think about. A guy and his girlfriend, who have been together for several months, are arguing. Again.

THIS time it's because he has cancelled their weekend plans three weekends in a row. Now, she seems to have a problem with much of what he does, but he's a good guy and he tries to ignore her arguing and complaining. His "boys" tell him that he's the one with the problem because he keeps dealing with her. He tries to explain that it isn't his fault because his work schedule keeps changing. She raises her voice and tells him that she doesn't believe him, and that he is probably seeing someone on the side. He tells her that if she doesn't believe him, she can come to his job and see that he's really at work. She responds by yelling that she knows he's lying because she heard that his ex-girlfriend is trying to get back together with him and that he probably still likes her.

With every remark she gets LOUDER! He tells her that she's crazy, and that he has something to do. He tries to walk away, but she blocks him from moving. Every time he tries to walk around her, she pushes him and puts her finger in his face while she is yelling at him. After a few more minutes of this he...

THINK ABOUT IT...

What do you think he does?

Let me help you with this one; he walks away. I mean he really walks away. He walks away from the whole relationship and keeps on going. After he tells her that he's done with her, do you think she stops the yelling and screaming?

Lesson 21

YOLO: WHAT MAKES YOU HAPPY?

It's not always easy to figure out what brings you the most happiness. Some adults can't even answer this question. That's because happiness can be a moving target. What makes a person happy today is not necessarily what will make him or her happy tomorrow. Finding it is a lifelong journey.

But if I know one thing for sure, it's this: Happiness exists on the inside, not the outside. The moment you define your happiness by who you know, what you have, or what you do, you have lost your ability to control your happiness. Why? Because you can't control anything outside of yourself. You can't make someone love you. You can't make someone want to be in a relationship with you. You can't control when someone you love dies. You can't determine when your employer may have to impose massive layoffs that may affect your job. You can't control what your friends may think about your decisions. You can't control whether you get accepted into the college that is your first pick.

All you can control is yourself, through your thoughts, actions, and decisions. YOLO: You only live once.

This doesn't mean you should make your life all about you. Everyone needs to have a supportive circle of friends and family, and ultimately, we all need each other. What I am saying is that if you are intensely needy and your happiness is linked to someone or some thing you won't be happy for long. As I stated in an earlier lesson, your definition of self should not be based on how many guys flirt with you or text you or take you out. And your happiness should never ever be determined by whether or not you have a boyfriend. If you only feel good about your life and yourself when you're in a relationship, then you're setting yourself up for a huge crash if you break up.

People will come and go in your life for any number of reasons. As we discussed in a previous lesson, sometimes individuals want more space to grow and explore different interests. Remember, you're still trying to figure yourself out while he is trying to understand himself. Both of you are at the beginning of your adult lives, so your period of discovery is just getting under way. What either of you may like today may be totally different in six months, and that's fine. Don't fight it ... go with it!

Keep in mind that we're living in a rapidly changing world where people are finding opportunities in other states, and even other countries. So, if you or your guy are finishing high school and preparing to go away to college, you will be learning about a new environment, and new people. A few relationships can endure the test of distance, but many do not. If you find yourself in a situation where there is physical space between you, you should not overlook opportunities that present themselves to you in your new world. If you are destined to be with the person you have left behind—or the person who has left you—only time will tell.

Find a healthy way to create joy within yourself. You can do that by loving yourself and setting limits on who you will allow to enter and remain in your precious world. If you have to spend time alone, so be it. Alone time presents a great opportunity to explore your fears, doubts and desires. In the process, you discover new interests and become better acquainted with the real you. You learn to respect yourself more and treat yourself with kindness.

And when you do that, guess what can happen? You attract a special, caring young man who seems as if he was meant to share his journey through life with a bright young lady who has herself together.

That young lady is you.

ACKNOWLEDGEMENTS

I want to thank my parents, LaBan M. Brown and Lillian Ruth Lewis Brown, for being supportive, visionary parents. I am able to offer sound guidance because of the women who have influenced my life:

My mother, who taught me that being happy is my entitlement, and that it does not have to be the result of having someone, nor should it come at anyone's expense.

My aunt, Esther McGhee, who taught me the importance of not allowing myself to be into someone who is not into me.

My childhood role model, Myra Anderson, who taught me the importance of being ladylike, elegant, and graceful, and that I don't have to raise my voice to be heard.

My cousin Dolores Lobbins, who taught me to be intolerant of men who show disrespect in any form, and to always have my look together, even when running short errands because you never know who you may encounter.

My friend Jean Brown, who taught me the importance of having a mystique.

My cousin Barbara Brown, who taught me the importance of managing situations logically rather than emotionally.

I thank my daughter, Ericka, for being the young woman you have become.

My sibling, Marie Brown, all I can say is thank you.

My cousin, Tara Miller, for sharing this journey with me.

Akil Alvin, whose talent is beyond measure.

Now, regarding the book itself, I owe gratitude to so many people, especially Denise Crittendon, who has been instrumental throughout, from inspiration through substantial contributions and on through completion, and Alex Cruden, my above-and-beyond editor. I thank the book's concept development committee for their engagement, rich discussions, honest feedback, and insights:

Che Baker, Kiondre Brooks, Jonathan Caldwell-Matthews, Celestle Christian, Cynthia Coble, Niya Cox, Amy Dickerson, Benjamin Dirden, Odette Duke, ReBecca Holland, Eunice Howard, Samantha Howard, Mahogany Jones, Tori Jones, Angelique Peterson-Mayberry, Brooklyn Peterson, Dwight McDonald, Jalon Nelson, Donnie Pruitt, Kevin Reeves, Ping Spells, Jessamine Wallington, Keirra Williams, and Yolanda Williams-Davis.

Thanks for their tremendous support for this project go to Debra Anderson, Joel Boykin, and Greg Dunmore of Pulsebeat Media, Devon Buskin, Madeline Escamille, Bernadette Elsey-Lewis, Shawn Jacque, Carol Lynn, Mary Henderson, Renee Henderson, Joy Lawrence, Beverly March, Maxine Mickens, Kim Moore, Beverly Morrison-Green, Vanessa Parnell, Brenda Peek, Kathryn Seabron, Sharon Strean, Curtis and Mildred Walton, Alicia Warren, Robbyn Williams, and Virginia 'Ginni' Winters.

Thank you to Crystal Larry and the Inn at 97 Winder in Detroit for providing a beautiful venue for book discussions.

And a special thank you to all the wonderful young people who have trusted my ability to offer them guidance, and who have enriched my life throughout the years.

If I have overlooked acknowledging anyone who has contributed to the process of bringing this book to life, please charge it to my head, and not my heart.

"Experience is the teacher of the Masters, but the fees are pretty high."

—My uncle, Nicholas Brown

www.ingramcontent.com/pod-product-compliance
Lightning Source LLC
Chambersburg PA
CBHW070043120526
44589CB00035B/2294